The Pigtail War

POINTS OF AMERICAN DIPLOMATIC
AND MILITARY INTEREST DURING
THE SINO-JAPANESE WAR OF 1894-1895

The Pigtail War:

American Involvement
in the Sino-Japanese War
of 1894–1895

Jeffery M. Dorwart

University of Massachusetts Press   Amherst   1975

Library of Congress Cataloging in Publication Data
Dorwart, Jeffery M. 1944–
   The Pigtail War: American involvement in the Sino-Japanese War
of 1894–1895.
   Bibliography: p.
   Includes index.
   1. United States—Foreign relations—East (Far East) 2. East
(Far East)—Foreign relations—United States. 3. Chinese-Japanese
War, 1894–1895. I. Title.
DS518.8.D65   327.73'05   75–8446
ISBN 0–87023–183–9

For Nel and Catherine

Illustrations

Contents

Preface

The Sino-Japanese War of 1894–1895 lies between two
periods of intense American diplomatic activity in East
Asia. Several decades before the war, the United States
established formal treaty relations with China and Japan.
In 1844 Caleb Cushing negotiated the Treaty of Wanghia
with China and won the same commercial and residency
privileges already granted to Great Britain as well as additional extraterritorial rights. Fourteen years later the Treaty
of Tientsin gave Westerners further access to trade and
travel prerogatives in China, while at the same time similar
arrangements with Japan pried open that country to Americans. In the period after the Sino-Japanese conflict, once
again the United States concentrated on East Asian affairs
and through the Open Door Notes of 1899 and 1900 em-
phasized its concern for equal access to Asian markets.
Encouraged by its victory over Spain and acquisition of the
Philippine Islands, the United States joined other great
powers in 1900 in military intervention to protect the Peking
legations against the Boxers. A few years later, Theodore
Roosevelt accelerated involvement in the Far East by medi-
ating the Russo-Japanese War of 1904–1905 and sending
the fleet to visit East Asian ports in 1907.

The interjacent years, though, marked the nadir of American interest in East Asia. Many diplomatic historians consider this interval unimportant in the development of policies
and attitudes toward the Far East and argue that the
United States remained aloof from Asian problems during
the 1880s and early 1890s. They often treat the period as
a gap between two more eventful and important stages of
American diplomacy toward East Asia. Despite this view,
the intervening years in fact witnessed considerable Amer-

Preface

ican diplomatic and even military activity in the area. During
the Franco-Chinese War of 1883–1884 and more fully during the Sino-Japanese War of 1894–1895 U.S. diplomacy
reaffirmed and strengthened earlier conduct in the Far East
and suggested new policies. The United States interfered in
both conflicts, offered good offices to mediate the wars and
restore order, rushed gunboats to the region to protect property and lives, promoted an open door policy, and outlined
a policy of neutrality. In the latter war, the government assumed far-reaching obligations and duties in East Asia and
landed troops on the Asian mainland to defend them.

This study focuses on American diplomacy toward the
Sino-Japanese War of 1894–1895. It examines the extent of
involvement in the conflict and attempts to discover the
motives behind increased governmental and public interest
in Eastern Asia during the war. Contemporary evaluations
of the controversy are surveyed, as are the contributions
of Secretary of State Walter Q. Gresham and President
Grover Cleveland to nineteenth-century East Asian diplomacy, including discussion of where the administration
strengthened existing policies and suggested new alterna-
tives. This history of the United States and the Sino-
Japanese War of 1894–1895 presumes that East Asian
considerations were an integral part of United States diplomacy during the second Cleveland administration and that
the war should be treated not only by scholars of East Asian
civilization and international relations but also by students
of American diplomatic history.

Many helped with the preparation of this book. Robert
H. Ferrell, Ernest R. May, and Louis L. Gerson read
various drafts and suggested revisions. When I became
discouraged with the study, Professors Howard H. Quint
and Reinhold A. Dowart, my father, encouraged me to continue and helped instill some discipline in my writing and
thinking. Malcolm Call, editor of the University of Massachusetts Press, provided help beyond that expected by any
author. Special thanks is reserved for my mentor Robert A.
Hart, a fine scholar, teacher, and warm human being.

Monroeville, New Jersey   JEFFERY M. DORWART
December 1974

1

Cleveland, Gresham, and East Asia

"Every nation, and especially every strong nation, must sometime be conscious of an impulse to rush into difficulties that do not concern it except in a highly imaginary way," American Secretary of State Walter Q. Gresham wrote to President Grover Cleveland on May 9, 1894. "To restrain the indulgence of such a propensity is not only the part of wisdom," Gresham continued, "but a duty we owe to the world as an example of the strength, the moderation, and the beneficence of popular government." [1] Gresham was referring to the expansionist Samoan policy of President Benjamin Harrison's administration which had entangled the United States in a joint occupation of those remote islands. The present government, he warned Cleveland, must never repeat Harrison's mistake and become involved in some distant overseas complication. But several months later a Korean rebellion and Sino-Japanese warfare, which endangered American lives in East Asia, focused the Cleveland regime's attention on the Far East. Though the government remained neutral during the Asian conflict of 1894–1895, American officials became entangled in Oriental spy cases, disputes over saving Asian lives, and peace negotiations. The president and his secretary of state landed troops in Korea, dispatched almost half of the U.S. Navy to Chinese waters, and readied soldiers for a march to Peking.

News of threats to American interests in East Asia surprised the Cleveland administration. Not since the Franco-Chinese War of 1883–1884 had the United States government interceded in East Asian affairs, and one had to return

to mid-century during the Anglo-French-Chinese controversies to discover serious intrusions into the area. In 1894
Americans expressed little concern for that relatively
unknown region of the world, and even those engaged in
the China trade watched as Russell and Company, the last
merchant house exchanging goods in China, discontinued
business. Missionaries continued to enter the mainland,
but with the absence of antiforeign outbreaks, religious
workers required less protection and the Navy Department
retained only one small cruiser and an unseaworthy gunboat
on the Asiatic Station. The State Department, meanwhile,
communicated infrequently with its representatives and
allowed legations and consular buildings to fall into
disrepair.

Cleveland and Gresham expected no change in this stable
situation. During his first term from 1885 to 1889, the
president had limited his interest in Asian diplomacy to
expressions of friendship and pledges of continued harmo-
nious relations with China, Japan, and Korea. Adjustment
of treaty arrangements with these countries had consumed
some time, but he had left the details up to Secretary of
State Thomas F. Bayard. Cleveland approached Asian relations during the early part of his second administration in a
similar manner. Discussions with China and Japan for
treaty revision dragged on, and the registration of Chinese
laborers in the United States under the Geary Act remained
a sensitive issue. But neither required undue concern, and
as the president told Congress in December 1893 recent
amendments to the Geary laws extended the allowed time
for registration and removed most of the opposition to
the restrictive measure.[2]

Cleveland's background and concentration on domestic
problems influenced his disregard of East Asian diplomacy.
The former mayor of Buffalo and governor of New York
had left the country twice, to go to Canada and to the West
Indies, and had rarely ventured west of the Mississippi
River. To the twenty-fourth president of the United States,
the Pacific Ocean and the Far East seemed a long way off.
Moreover, he could not pay attention to such a remote

place when more immediate, familiar, and urgent issues of domestic politics piled up on his desk. During the months when unrest and violence in East Asia first forced his administration to look to China and Korea, the president confronted the darkest and most difficult days of his life. The Pullman strike, struggle over the tariff, fights for civil service reform, and attempts to preserve a sound gold currency all coincided with the outbreak of Asian warfare during the summer of 1894. Cleveland also contended with a severe economic depression, agrarian unrest, and social discontent. The president might have looked to Asian markets during this period to help alleviate the country's economic ills, but he did not. Instead he turned his back on the growing Asian crisis.

Grover Cleveland's view of foreign affairs reinforced his desire to avoid Asian complications. He deplored the belligerent tones of the previous administration when Harrison and Secretary of State James G. Blaine had pursued one of the more aggressive policies since the Civil War. They had kindled war scares with Italy brought about by a dispute over the lynching of eleven Italians in New Orleans and with Chile when a Valparaiso mob murdered two American sailors on shore leave. Harrison had sympathized with advocates of American expansion and had eagerly embraced Hawaiian annexationists. Cleveland determined to return to a less enthusiastic and dangerous foreign policy. His administration planned to apply a high standard of honor and morality to its international relations. The rotund chief executive promised an overseas program based on "conscience, justice, peace and neutrality," while "rejecting any share in foreign broils and ambitions upon other continents." [3]

Cleveland's secretary of state, Walter Q. Gresham, shared the president's conception of foreign policy. The appointment of this sad-eyed and bewhiskered Indiana native to the top cabinet post startled the most seasoned political observers. Gresham, a lifelong Republican and novice in foreign affairs, had served President Chester A. Arthur as postmaster general and secretary of the treasury and had been considered for his party's presidential nomination in

1888. Then, in 1892, he clashed with Harrison's Indiana political machine over voting frauds and bribery. The corruption disgusted Gresham, a man noted for his integrity and morality as evidenced by his attack on the notorious Louisiana lottery during the Arthur administration. The former judge broke with the Republicans, and the Populist Party asked him to become its presidential candidate. But Gresham, a sound money man, opposed the new party's free-silver platform and distrusted its apparent radicalism. He refused to become the standard-bearer for the Populists and instead backed Grover Cleveland, a leader esteemed for his civil service reform and honesty in government.[4]

Gresham explained his decision to friends. His animosity toward Harrison had not influenced him, he insisted, but Cleveland's support of tariff reduction and opposition to imperial expansion determined the way he would vote.[5] After the Democratic victory, Gresham prepared to retire from national politics. "I have no political ambition," he wrote Joseph Medill of the *Chicago Tribune,* "but if I had, no one realizes better than I do that I have committed political suicide." [6] On January 25, 1893, though, he received an unexpected offer from the president-elect asking him to become the secretary of state in the new administration. Cleveland respected this principled individual, appreciated his political support, and determined to find a cabinet position for him. When former Secretary of State Bayard and other close advisers refused the State Department portfolio, Cleveland offered it to Gresham.

The news astonished Gresham, who felt he might be suitable for a seat on the Supreme Court but not as director of the diplomatic organization. He feared accusations of an immoral deal and hesitated to accept the honor. Cleveland expected this response: "I beg you to believe that your sturdy regard for political duty and your supreme sincerity and disinterestedness, seen and known of all men, are proof against any and all unworthy suspicious or malicious criticism." [7] He asked Gresham to delay his final answer until Don Dickinson of Michigan, Cleveland's close aide and political manager, arrived at Gresham's Chicago residence to discuss the appointment. But despite the president-elect's assurances and Dickinson's personal appeal, Gresham declined the offer. He knew little about foreign affairs and, besides, wished to retire from public life and devote some time to his family.

Cleveland begged the former judge to reconsider his decision, and other cabinet nominations asked him to accept. At last he consented but informed Cleveland, "I still entertain misgivings, however, as to the wisdom of the step, but I hope that neither of us will ever have cause to regret it." [8] The president-elect disregarded this fear. There was no need for concern since the two men held identical views on the necessity for a sound gold standard, a lower tariff schedule, and the maintenance of law and order. They also shared the same idealistic notion of foreign relations, where policy must be guided by principle, morality, and respect for other nations, rather than by blatant self-interest and the acquisition of overseas territory, bases, or spheres of influence. As Gresham observed, "A free government cannot pursue an imperial policy. We acquire territory with the sole expectation of bringing it into the Union as a State, the equal of the other States." [9]

Several days after accepting the top diplomatic post, Gresham met with Cleveland and Treasury-designate John G. Carlisle, a square-faced, friendly Kentuckian, at the former's residence in Lakewood, New Jersey. The trio, who soon became close comrades, discussed the possibility of a financial panic in the country and the issuance of bonds to keep enough gold in the U.S. Treasury. Then talk turned to foreign policy, and the three agreed that Hawaiian annexation remained the outstanding diplomatic issue confronting the new administration. They did not, however, reach a decision on how the government would treat American possession of the Pacific islands. Though Hawaiian policy had not been defined at Lakewood, Gresham left the meeting certain of his opinions on the subject. The United States must not annex the remote territory, he believed, because "if we acquire Hawaii, we must defend Honolulu just as we would any of our Atlantic and Pacific ports." [10]

Secretary Gresham took charge of the State Department in March 1893 and set out at once to formulate a correct and humane policy toward Hawaii. The question of annexation had arisen during the last days of the preceding Harrison administration. In January 1893 the Hawaiian queen, Liliuokalani, had been dethroned by revolutionary forces reportedly backed by American sugar plantation owners and the American minister in Honolulu, John C. Stevens. Several weeks later representatives of the new government arrived in Washington to negotiate an annexation pact, and President Harrison and Secretary of State John W. Foster drew up a treaty on February 14, 1893. This document lay before the Senate when Cleveland and Gresham assumed office.[11]

Though not completely opposed to annexation, Cleveland acquiesced when his secretary of state urged delay and called for a careful investigation of the situation. On March 11 the administration sent former Georgia congressman, James H. Blount, to the islands, where he discovered that the majority of Hawaiians did not want annexation. At the same time rumors of illegal intervention, diplomatic fraud, and mistreatment of the Hawaiian queen reached Gresham. He was not surprised by the intelligence since he felt that anything Harrison touched became corrupt and immoral. The secretary asked Cleveland to abandon annexation and restore the poor woman to her throne. The president agreed and explained his position to Congress in December 1893. "Upon the facts developed it seemed to me the only course for our Government to pursue was to undo the wrong that had been done by those representing us and to restore as far as practicable the status existing at the time of our forcible intervention." [12]

Despite public declaration against annexation, in private Cleveland expressed reservations. Withdrawing the treaty was a mistake, he told William Shaw Bowen of the *New York World,* but he had to stand by his promise to Gresham.[13] The failure of the secretary's impossible crusade to restore Queen Liliuokalani gave the president further cause to regret his decision, and he finally asked

Congress to settle the Hawaiian question. He admitted his government's inability to resolve the problem and blamed the dilemma on Harrison and expansionist Republicans who had manufactured this crisis. The opposition naturally struck back and campaigned against the present administration's foreign policy. They cited the mishandling of Hawaiian annexation as evidence of how a weak, vacillating, and isolationist regime betrayed American national interests. These partisan attacks continued throughout Cleveland's entire second term and influenced his response to East Asian problems.[14]

Gresham's initial venture into diplomacy outside of the Western Hemisphere failed and forced the president to surrender leadership in Hawaiian affairs to Congress. In order to develop a realistic policy toward the disturbances now brewing in the Far East, the secretary needed guidance from department personnel familiar with the area. But he found the tiny State Department staff already overworked. Seventy-four bureau chiefs, clerks, and messengers dealt with a multitude of complex overseas issues. Staff size, bureau organization, and department procedure had changed little since the days of Secretary of State Hamilton Fish during the Grant era. Though typewriters and electricity had recently been installed in department offices, most business followed the familiar course from clerks copying notes by hand to messengers trundling back and forth between bureaus. The secretary and his assistants still spent long hours poring over the increasing number of diplomatic dispatches, while the Bureau of Indexes and Archives employed only eleven people to open mail, prepare and index abstracts of all correspondence, arrange papers for Congress, answer calls for documents, and run the archives. The State Department offices shared floor space with the War and Navy Departments in an old building located on 17th Street and Pennsylvania Avenue. Complaints of fine sand and dust which blew up through office windows from the unpaved streets outside and settled on the wet ink of government documents accented the cluttered and primitive atmosphere.[15]

In 1894 only two men in the State Department had the background and training to provide needed direction in East Asian diplomacy, Second Assistant Secretary of State Alvey A. Adee and Third Secretary William W. Rockhill. Adee, a walking encyclopedia of diplomatic information, had been in the department since 1877. He remembered where every dispatch had been filed and would be the man to consult for earlier approaches to Asian problems and for established policy procedures. But Adee was a loner, who considered the department his personal domain and in times of crisis set up a cot in his office and slept there overnight. When not taking long solitary bicycle rides through the still pristine Washington countryside or canoeing alone down the Potomac River, this eccentric figure jealously guarded the corridors, archive rooms, and files of the State Department and avoided the socially active secretary. The scarlet fever which permanently impaired Adee's hearing made it difficult for him to converse with Gresham, who was often accused of jumping rapidly from one subject to another and then forgetting what the original problem had been. The two men never were close and Gresham apparently did not often ask Adee's advice.[16]

William W. Rockhill served as the department's only recognized Asian expert in 1894. He had traveled widely in the Far East, had studied Oriental art and literature, and had established close contacts with many old China hands. This urbane scholar-diplomat had been a secretary at the U.S. legation in Peking from 1884 to 1889 and had also served in the Korean legation at Seoul. The athletic man, once a soldier in the French Foreign Legion and a trail hand in the wild New Mexico Territory, strode through the department, carefully groomed and supremely self-confident. He stood over six feet tall and sported a natty red mustache, providing a stark contrast to the elderly, often disheveled secretary of state. Gresham walked with a limp, the result of an old Civil War wound, and worked in the humid Washington air in rolled-up shirt sleeves. Rockhill never respected this informal and seemingly broken man. Furthermore, he coveted the Peking ministerial post and resented Gresham's close friend Charles Denby, then U.S. minister to China. He also disagreed with his chief's basic philosophy of foreign policy, sharing instead the expansionist sentiments of administration opponents. Rockhill numbered Theodore Roosevelt and Henry Cabot Lodge, two gentlemen who thoroughly disliked Gresham, among his intimate companions. He never discussed the Far East in any great detail with his boss, and Gresham disregarded the younger man's expertise.[17]

Gresham had to learn about East Asia from sources outside the State Department. Fortunately, fellow Hoosier and family friend, Colonel Charles Denby, remained the minister to China. "I wish all the States of the Union were full of such men," Gresham wrote Ambassador Bayard in London, and he expected to receive guidance here.[18] The Peking post had become the personal and highly profitable (Denby's $12,000 per year salary made him a better paid official than even the secretary, who drew an $8,000 annual salary) bailiwick of Charles Denby. This tired-looking Civil War veteran and ardent Cleveland man had received the China legation in 1885 as a reward for political service. Benjamin Harrison, another Indiana son, had left Denby in office, and by 1894 the sixty-five-year-old minister resident lived comfortably in the Chinese capital. He had brought over Princeton-educated Charles Jr., one of eight Denby children, as his assistant and groomed the young man to succeed him. Though Denby could be relied upon for advice on China policy, in 1894 he had returned to the United States for a kidney stone operation, leaving his son in charge of the legation at this critical period in East Asian history.[19]

With his father temporarily on leave, Acting Minister Denby hoped to impress Washington with his ability to direct the four-man legation. The younger diplomat possessed some knowledge of Chinese language and culture, but he was inexperienced, vain, and refused to listen to opinion from his senior colleagues, particularly legation interpreter Duncan Fleming Cheshire. Cheshire had been in China for over twenty-five years and had served at the

Foochow, Canton, and Shanghai consulates before coming to Peking. But despite Cheshire's familiarity with China, the youthful Denby never consulted him. Cheshire had his own ambitions for the ministerial post and wrote a number of letters to State Department crony Rockhill belittling young Denby and complaining about his disregard of the seasoned interpreter's advice. This rivalry, combined with Denby's efforts to convince Washington of his mastery of legation business, made the acting minister hesitate to reveal problems in Peking which might reflect his inexperience. Thus, Gresham could not count on accurate information or mature advice from the American legation in China.[20]

Other American ministers in East Asia provided insufficient additional help in the secretary's search for counsel on a proper policy in the Far East. Edwin Dun, sent to Japan in 1873 as an agricultural expert, represented the government in Tokyo. He had remained in the island country, had married a Japanese, and by 1893 had worked his way from second secretary of the legation to become U.S. minister to Japan. Though a long-time resident of Japan, Dun provided limited insight into Japanese diplomacy, and his unimaginative, factual dispatches added nothing to the State Department's understanding of the region. Dun's real interest lay in experimental farming and stockbreeding, not diplomacy.[21] John M. B. Sill, a stocky, bearded former superintendent of Detroit public schools and part of the Michigan clique headed by Don Dickinson and Assistant Secretary of State Edwin F. Uhl, filled the Korean post. Sill became a vigorous defender of American interests in Korea, but his stubborn disregard of departmental instructions and his feud with another Rockhill intimate, missionary-diplomat and legation secretary Horace N. Allen, limited his effectiveness and reliability in Washington's eyes.[22]

American consuls in the area shared many of the same doubtful qualifications as their superiors. Despite attempts at civil service reform at the consular level by Cleveland and Assistant Secretary of State Josiah Quincy until 1894, and later by Edwin F. Uhl, consulships were still distributed as political rewards and not on the basis of professional ability. Cleveland, in fact, changed 117 consuls in 1894 alone, most for purely political reasons.[23] Aggressive, ambitious young men such as Tientsin consul Sheridan Pitt Read used every available political connection to win a diplomatic appointment and then, once at their post, grasped for power and influence. These consuls often slanted dispatches to Washington, promoted their own careers, and clouded actual East Asian conditions. This was particularly dangerous in Read's case since he was situated near the Chinese capital and relied upon to provide an accurate evaluation of local conditions. Though Read did send informative dispatches, the Department could not always expect judicious and impartial reports from a consul who used self-serving cables to promote a diplomatic career. Moreover, it later suspected Read of illegal financial activities in China and disregarded intelligence from this supposed unsavory character.[24]

Personality conflicts, communication problems, and the lack of professional diplomats at home and abroad restricted the diplomatic establishment's usefulness as a source of direction and information for the novice secretary of state in the field of East Asian relations. Even the latest relevant literature proved no more helpful in understanding Oriental politics than Gresham's other sources of information. Reports from missionaries, journalists, and general travelers created an image of mystery surrounding the strange world, while books and articles stressed the exotic and unusual. East Asia seemed a land of cruel warlords, opium dens, heathen temples, and masses of unwashed coolies. "The streets are teeming with dust, dirt, or slush, and crowded day and night with a ceaseless flow of indigent, but, so far as one can see, contented human beings, all busily engaged in the sordid struggle of life," Delaware businessman James Harrison Wilson, a visitor to the Far East, wrote in his popular book on China. "It is all inconceivably squalid and offensive to foreign eyes and nostrils, and fills the foreign soul with a sentiment of unutterable disgust." [25] Reading such current accounts of Asia did not enlighten Gresham.

Newspaper descriptions reaching Washington in early

1894 perpetuated this theme. The most widely read narratives came from the pen of syndicated columnist Frank George Carpenter, a tiny, bespectacled man with homely features and a penchant for the bizarre and unknown. Carpenter toured China, Japan, and Korea in 1894 and examined Asian life in great detail, visiting prisons, palaces, and villages. Korean society, in particular, fascinated him, and he explained to American readers the common practice of paddling, whereby a prisoner's skin was torn from his body. He interviewed Korea's "squeezers," officials who made millions by taxing an already impoverished people. The reporter traveled through the countryside and visited rich gold mines used only to provide trinkets for the royal family. Calling the Asian monarchy "queer old Corea," Carpenter portrayed the Hermit Kingdom as a land of Oriental mystery, strange almond-eyed beauties, and grotesque tortures.[26]

With few Asian experts at his disposal and confronted by an impression of some exotic world full of barbaric peoples, Secretary Gresham faced growing trouble in the Far East. He first focused attention on Korea in early 1894. This tiny, insignificant kingdom had become the object of international rivalries in East Asia and a battleground between China and Japan. Rooted deeply in the past, the Sino-Japanese struggle for control of the peninsula at last had reached its climax. Japan's rapid modernization during the past decades brought her into direct confrontation with China and Russia. Many Japanese statesmen favored a gradual and measured approach to power, preferring diplomacy rather than war to strengthen their economic and political position in Korea and to revise their hated extraterritorial treaties with Western nations. When a Japanese-backed Korean rebellion failed in 1884, diplomats had outmaneuvered a pro-Chinese faction through the Li-Ito Convention signed at Tientsin the following year. The Tientsin pact not only indemnified Japan for her property destroyed during the abortive insurrection but also indirectly acknowledged China's recognition of Japan's equal status in Korea.[27]

Russian plans to build a trans-Siberian railway and growing European imperialism in East Asia, however, complicated Japan's gradualist policies and gave strength to militant spokesmen. By 1894 these leaders had forced several dissolutions of the Japanese Diet, and some predicted that the violent debates would lead to a revolution, while others believed that only a great overseas adventure could bring the divided country together. Then in the spring of 1894 the murder of a pro-Japanese Korean political refugee, Kim Ok-kyun, and the rebellion of a fanatical nationalist sect called Tonghak provided the opportunity for such advocates of an aggressive foreign policy.[28]

The Chinese forced Kim to leave Korea after the abortive uprising of 1884, and he escaped to Tokyo where he became an agent for further Japanese intervention in peninsular politics. In late March 1894 a supposed friend lured Kim to a Japanese hotel in the International Settlement at Shanghai and assassinated him. Almost at once a Chinese gunboat transported the body back to Korea where the local government publicly dismembered it and displayed the parts throughout the provinces. The Chinese added further insult to the Japanese by treating Kim's killer as a patriotic national hero and by encouraging Korean agents to murder other pro-Japanese politicians and refugees.[29]

While the Kim affair increased Japan's hatred for China and stirred up the war party, an insurrection by Tonghak furnished the catalyst for a Sino-Japanese conflict. Founded in 1860 by Korean prophet Ch'oe Che-u, the organization preached a doctrine which drew liberally from Buddhism, Taoism, Confucianism, and even Christianity. Ch'oe called the movement Tonghak or Eastern Learning, and though the Korean government executed him as a rebel in 1864 and drove the sect underground, his disciples kept its spirit alive. In 1893 it reappeared with political and nationalistic overtones to protest the corruption and taxation policies of the Korean government in Seoul. The revitalized Tonghak blamed foreign influence for Korea's problems, and its banners called for the reorganization of society on the principle of Confucian virtue, the elimination of Japanese barbarians, and the extermination of corrupt nobles and officials. When King Kojong, twenty-sixth ruler of Chosŏn, ignored Tonghak petitions, the cult rebelled and dragged most of the southern provinces into the insurrection. By May 1894 the rebels threatened the capital, and the king, coerced by Yuan Shih-kai, Chinese consul in Seoul, asked China for assistance in quelling the disturbance. Japan, citing the joint action provision of the 1885 Tientsin convention, also responded by sending cavalry, artillery, and infantry into Korea. Large bodies of Chinese and Japanese soldiers now faced each other on the Korean peninsula, and both refused to withdraw their forces.[30]

King Kojong looked for assistance to prevent a clash of the two Asian giants on his territory. The beleaguered monarch summoned his closest Western adviser, American medical missionary and diplomat Horace N. Allen, to the palace. Allen, who acted more like a shrewd bureaucrat than a religious worker, had arrived in Korea a decade before and had become entangled in Korean factional struggles, court intrigues, and international rivalries almost from his first day in the strange kingdom. The red-haired Ohioan earned the royal family's gratitude by saving the life of the queen's nephew who had suffered severe sword wounds when attacked by an assassin. The missionary's medicine amazed the inquisitive young king, and he asked Allen to tell him more about the Western world. Friendship between the two grew, and soon the American visited Kojong almost daily, discussed Korea's problems with the king, and in 1887 even set up a legation for him in Washington. Now, seven years later, as troops massed in his nation, Kojong turned once again to his American comrade for counsel. The missionary, who had promoted increased American influence on the peninsula for years, advised the king to request U.S. intermediation.[31]

Allen anticipated sympathy for Korea in the United States because the Korean-American Treaty of 1882, the first with a Western nation, called for arbitration if any power acted unjustly toward either country. The pact also ignored China's tributary relations with Korea under which

China provided protection in return for control over Korean politics. The United States sent a fully accredited minister to Seoul in 1887 and agreed to provide military instructors for the kingdom's tiny army, though American support for Korean independence never amounted to anything more than moral suasion.[32]

After his conversation with Kojong, Allen convinced the new U.S. minister, John M. B. Sill, to request Washington's intervention. Conditions endangered American lives and required military protection, the veteran missionary insisted. Sill, a strong-willed man who deplored Allen's intimacy with the distraught king and later challenged the Ohioan's leadership, agreed to apply for a warship. The minister had been in Korea only a few weeks and had no reason to question Allen's motives. Sill cabled Rear Admiral Joseph S. Skerrett, commander of the U.S. Navy on the Asiatic Station, and asked if a man-of-war might be sent to the Korean harbor at Chemulpo (Inchon).[33]

Sill's request disturbed Admiral Skerrett, a crotchety and conservative old officer only months away from retirement. He had comfortable rooms in Nagasaki and had brought his wife and lovely daughter over to Japan to share his remaining time in the service. Skerrett did not wish to be disturbed by a few missionaries in Korea and, more importantly, knew that he had only one effective cruiser, *Baltimore,* to patrol the entire station. His other available vessel, a Civil War vintage, side-wheeled gunboat, *Monocacy,* was considered unseaworthy by its captain, Robert E. Impey. Commander Impey opposed any journey into the rough waters around Korea and kept his vessel tied to a Tientsin dock.[34] Other American warships steamed in the Bering Sea and required weeks to reinforce Skerrett's ships. With these limited resources at his disposal, he turned down Sill's request for a ship. These local disturbances in Korea usually burned themselves out, the officer assured Sill, and local authorities could take care of the situation.[35]

Skerrett, considered by some a "travesty in the American navy," put personal comfort above concern for missionaries in Korea but also understood the limitations of the navy in

East Asia. His dilemma reflected the woeful state of the American fleet in 1894. The United States ranked far below the major sea powers—England, France, Germany, Italy, and Russia—in all types of warships. It even trailed Argentina, Brazil, Chile, Denmark, Holland, Turkey, Japan, and China in numbers of small, fast torpedo and gun boats. The Navy Department had nineteen modern cruisers and gunboats and a handful of obsolete vessels available for the varied responsibilities of the North Atlantic, South Atlantic, European, Pacific, and Asiatic stations.[36] The navy had more than a dozen fine ships under construction which gradually replaced the decrepit wooden boats and low draft monitors of the Civil War years with modern steel ships, but in 1894 the new cruisers and first battleships still were undergoing preliminary trials and were unavailable for naval duty. The United States simply did not have enough vessels to protect the many missionary stations and treaty ports in East Asia and still leave adequate warships for other assignments.

Navy Department problems did not interest Horace Allen in Korea, and he would not be put off by a naval officer. When Allen learned about Skerrett's refusal to send a ship to Chemulpo, he utilized other channels to bring an American cruiser to Korea. Influential contacts in Washington, especially W. W. Rockhill, could be employed if necessary, but first he visited Kojong and repeated advice for Korea to demand a gunboat to restore order and protect lives. On June 1, 1894, the monarch wired his minister in Washington, asking him to beg for a man-of-war. The Cleveland administration could not ignore an appeal from a legitimate government having formal treaty relations with the United States. This was the first formal contact with the Asian disturbance of 1894 and began Gresham's frantic search for information. The secretary ambled down the corridor of his office building to the Navy Department. After discussing the question with Secretary of the Navy Hilary A. Herbert of Alabama, another disabled Civil War veteran, Gresham inquired "whether a vessel may conveniently be sent to that point for the protection of our Legation and citizens of the

United States residing there and to express the hope of the Department that this course may be followed if practicable." [37]

The final decision to send a warship to Korea, of course, rested with the president. On June 2 Cleveland called in Assistant Secretary of the Navy William McAdoo, a former New Jersey congressman and member of the Committee on Naval Affairs, to discover the department's position on the situation. McAdoo told the president that Skerrett's flagship *Baltimore,* famous for nearly starting a war with Chile under the previous administration, rode at anchor only forty-eight hours away from Chemulpo. Cleveland delayed. He had promised to tone down Harrison's foreign policies, and strikes, tariff revision, and domestic unrest already plagued him. Administration critics attacked his Hawaiian policy, and intervention several months before in the Brazilian Revolution had almost led to a naval battle. Should his government become involved in Korea as well?

Cleveland decided to send *Baltimore* to Korea. Moved not by expectations of promoting the insignificant American trade with Korea but by an emotional concern for the missionaries in the area, the president acted. He held a special affection for these overseas religious workers since his oldest sister had married a missionary and had gone off to work in Asia (Ceylon). He was "one of the strongest advocates I have ever known of the missionary cause," the president's friend and biographer George F. Parker later wrote. Cleveland, the son of a Presbyterian minister, knew that a number of American missionaries resided in Korea; in fact, on the very day that he decided to rush a warship to the trouble spot, the morning papers had reported that several hundred Christian apostles were in grave danger. Actually no more than eighty missionaries resided in Korea in 1894, but the president determined to defend any number.[38]

Baltimore reached Chemulpo from Nagasaki in early June 1894. Not as impressive as some of the larger European warships in the area, the 4,413-ton flagship of the Asiatic Station nevertheless made a fine show. Built by William Cramps and Sons of Philadelphia and commissioned in 1890, *Baltimore* carried a crew of 36 officers and 350 men. Armed with a variety of breech-loading rifles and rapid-firing guns, the 327-foot cruiser gave the U.S. Navy one of its best fighting ships then available, and its presence undoubtedly impressed Westerners and Asians alike. Minister Sill believed *Baltimore*'s timely arrival restored order around Seoul. The rebellion collapsed because of the "salutary moral effect" of the warship, he wrote Washington. The government released Sill's cable to the press, and one enthusiastic editor insisted that the cruiser's appearance and the "spreading of the stars and stripes over helpless people" had "indirectly assisted the [Korean] government by the moral effect of the ship's presence at a critical juncture." [39]

The Tonghak rebellion, though hardly suppressed, no longer presented the major problem to the Korean government or to Americans on the peninsula. Instead, the involvement of Chinese and Japanese soldiers became the main issue. The Japanese rapidly occupied the roads to Seoul, fortified their positions, and increased their legation guard. At the same time, Chinese troop transports rushed reinforcements to Korea. Neither side appeared willing to compromise or retreat. Apprehensive dispatches reached Washington from American legations in Seoul and Tokyo, warning the Cleveland government to pay careful attention to developments in the Far East. Minister Dun in Japan cited Japan's intransigence and discussed the issue with Japanese Foreign Minister Mutsu Munemitsu. Imperial troops, Mutsu informed Dun, merely protected property and lives and would not provoke war. The American diplomat expressed doubt. "It is impossible to believe that so large a force is required in Korea for the protection of Japan's legation, consulates and subjects," Dun wrote Gresham on June 15, "inasmuch as she already has in Korean ports ten ships of war." [40] Sill shared Dun's concern and questioned Japan's "ulterior purpose" in sending thousands of soldiers to the peninsula. The Korean king also feared the Japanese and asked Sill for asylum in the American legation if Japan attacked Seoul.[41]

While Dun and Sill warned their government about

Japan's potential aggression, back in Washington the Japanese minister to the United States, Tateno Gozo, countered with his own arguments and presented his regime's case to Assistant Secretary of State Uhl. China's stubborn position and not Japan's had created the serious confrontation in Korea, and China, still insisting that Korea was a tributary state, refused to recognize the equality of other nations in the region. Moreover, backward China prevented the development of Korean industry, commerce, and transportation, while crushing any attempts at social reform and supporting a corrupt and reactionary government. Japan would not withdraw its forces from Korea, Tateno concluded, until China joined it in a program of economic and administrative reform for the crumbling Hermit Kingdom.[42]

As tension increased the Cleveland administration became concerned that the outbreak of war would endanger American lives and might lead to some unwanted involvement in East Asian fighting. Displaying an unusual interest and uncharacteristic leadership in Asian diplomacy, Cleveland employed American diplomacy to prevent armed conflict on the peninsula which would upset the status quo. "In the view of the friendly interest of the United States in the welfare of Korea and its people," Assistant Secretary Uhl cabled Sill on July 22, "you are by direction of the President instructed to use every possible effort for the preservation of peaceful conditions." [43] Cleveland assumed sole responsibility for this approach. Gresham vacationed away from Washington, and as the president later lectured Congress, "I felt constrained at the beginning of the controversy to tender our good offices to induce an amicable arrangement of the Japanese demands for administrative reforms in Korea." [44]

Sill misunderstood the sudden interest in Korean affairs and believed the president's personal involvement meant that he considered peace in East Asia a major concern of the U.S. government. An ordained minister and loyal Democrat who admired the virtuous man in the White House, Sill accepted Cleveland's instructions without reservations and resolved to do his best to preserve order. It mattered little to Sill that the president held only a vague idea of conditions far over the Pacific Ocean where Imperial China plotted to entangle the United States in the controversy, through its policy of using barbarians to control barbarians. The Chinese had already applied for Russian mediation of Sino-Japanese differences and had asked Great Britain, France, and the United States to preserve order.[45]

Cleveland's instructions coincided with other efforts to avoid war and, though formulated independently, appeared to advance a policy of joint intervention in Korea. Hence, Sill cooperated with what he called Caucasian representatives in Korea when they pressed China and Japan to withdraw troops from the area. The United States had followed the European lead before, benefiting from the unequal treaty system as a most favored nation, and Sill considered collaboration with British, French, and Russian agents consistent with the president's orders to use every possible effort to preserve peace. Besides, the Korean king had begged the United States to adjust the difficulty, and the United States had treaty obligations to uphold. Sill also hoped to avert bloodshed by providing asylum for Korean officials in the American legation and by keeping *Baltimore* in Chemulpo harbor.[46]

The president's initial venture into East Asian diplomacy threatened to compromise an independent policy and promised association with entangling alliances. At this point Gresham returned to his office and assumed direction of American peace efforts in Korea. His unfamiliarity with Far Eastern affairs, as well as his mismanagement of Hawaiian policy, made him hesitate to become involved in the Korean question, but he recognized the dangers inherent in the Cleveland-Sill approach to the peninsula. Minister Stevens in Hawaii had already revealed what an overly enthusiastic minister could do with a local rebellion, and Gresham wished to avoid similar embarrassments with Minister Sill. This concern overcame his timidity, and he seized the initiative for guiding Asian policy by issuing a public statement on the current unrest in the Far East. "The United States did not exercise any protectorate over Korea," he declared, and "the most this Government could do in any event would be to tender its offices to settle the difficulty." [47] This statement was far more restrained than the president's order to use every possible effort to preserve peaceful conditions.

Though still an amateur diplomat, Secretary Gresham suspected sinister and immoral forces behind Korea's pleas for assistance, and he paused before rushing headlong into the fray. He soon abandoned caution, though, after a conversation with Minister Tateno. Hoping to learn more about the situation, Gresham summoned the Japanese diplomat to his private study in the State Department. Gresham asked Tateno why Japan had sent so many soldiers to Korea and when they would be removed. The troops had been sent to protect Japanese lives and property, Tateno responded, and would leave only after Korea made necessary domestic reforms. Disclaiming any American intent to intervene, Gresham wondered if Japan would respect Korean independence. The minister replied that Japan had no territorial ambitions on the peninsula. The secretary, an accomplished lawyer used to cross-examining witnesses, paused and then looked straight at Tateno. "I suppose, Mr. Minister, your Government is watching China more than Korea, and that you are looking to war more with the former than you are with the latter?" Tateno answered at once. "That is correct. Our situation at home is critical, and war with China would improve it by arousing the patriotic sentiment of our people and more strongly attaching them to the Government." [48]

Tateno's admission that Japan willingly risked a great Asian conflagration to restore domestic order upset Gresham. Torn between a reluctance to become involved in the distant incident and a sense of legal and moral obligations toward Korea, he decided to appeal to the Japanese government and ask it to cease this dangerous and immoral advance. On July 7 he instructed Dun to present the following message to the Japanese:

> The government of the United States has heard with sincere regret that although the insurrection has been suppressed and peace prevails in Korea, Japan refuses to withdraw her troops and demands that radical

changes be made in the domestic administration of Korea.

This demand is more remarkable in view of the fact that China favors the simultaneous withdrawal of both the Japanese and Chinese troops. Cherishing sincere friendship for both Japan and Korea, the United States indulge the hope that Korea's independence and sovereignty will be respected. You are instructed to say to the Government at Tokyo that the President will be painfully disappointed should Japan visit upon her feeble and defenceless neighbor the horrors of an unjust war.[49]

A more experienced secretary might not have issued such an intemperate and hastily written statement, full of innuendo and moral chagrin. Based on his conversation with Tateno, Gresham had judged Japan guilty in Korea and held her accountable for the entire Asian controversy. He defined the crisis simply in terms of good against evil or moral versus immoral interest groups. Apparently the secretary had not learned a lesson from the Hawaiian fiasco where he had made similar charges against opponents of the defenseless queen for their unjust rebellion.

The substance of Gresham's cablegram leaked to the press, and partisan editors attacked the secretary. On July 18 a Hearst editorial in the *San Francisco Examiner,* a critic of Cleveland's timid overseas policy and antiimperialism, accused Gresham of a grave diplomatic blunder in sending his accusatory note to Japan. The bumbling secretary had opposed Japan's legitimate attempt to drive barbaric China out of Korea and open backward nations to civilization, the West Coast paper suggested, because his friendship for the Chinese minister in Washington, Yang Ju, had blinded him to China's own aggression. The muckraking journal alleged further that Yang had secured Gresham's sympathies for China by bribing him with expensive gifts. Whitelaw Reid, editor of the *New York Tribune* and Benjamin Harrison's vice-presidential running mate in 1892, added more abuse, calling Gresham a meddler and willing dupe of the sly and unscrupulous Oriental diplomat. Other Republican and expansionist editors reflected Reid's leadership, and as one New England daily concluded: "It is plain that if Secretary Gresham has without any provocation abruptly taken sides with Russia and China he has committed an act which can only be adequately described by saying that he has made an ass of himself in the State Department." [50]

Press criticism always bothered the sensitive secretary, and for several days he refused comment on his Asian policy. Rapidly disintegrating peace and order in Korea, however, forced his attention back to the trouble spot. In mid-July Japanese soldiers humiliated the British consul and his wife as they traveled near Seoul. Sill asked Washington to join London in demanding an apology for this affront to all Western powers. Gresham refused to become involved and ordered Dun not to permit Sill's criticism to reach the Japanese government.[51] Then on July 22 Japanese warriors forced their way into the Seoul palace and imprisoned Kojong. The streets of the capital filled with fleeing refugees, many of whom begged for sanctuary in the tiny American legation compound. Japanese soldiers remained the only force capable of preserving order and protecting property, Sill cabled Gresham, but reliance on this group to defend U.S. interests constituted collusion with the Japanese invaders. Instead, he called for a marine guard from *Baltimore,* anchored a few miles away in Chemulpo harbor.[52]

Benjamin F. Day, captain of the warship, resisted Sill's request for the landing of troopers on Korean soil. The idea of risking his men for the sake of a few foolhardy missionaries and an overwrought minister did not appeal to the fifty-three-year-old career officer any more than it had to Skerrett a month before. Little danger existed, Day wrote Sill, as long as the American community attended to its own affairs, and he rejected the petition for a guard.[53] Though furious, Sill refused to debate with Day and cabled Washington for assistance. If Japanese soldiers were allowed to protect Americans, the minister informed Gresham, China would regard it as an unfriendly act. The United States government, convinced by Sill's argument, ordered a marine watch to the Korean capital.[54]

On the evening of July 23, nearly fifty heavily armed marines and sailors under the command of Captain of Marines George F. Elliott left *Baltimore* for duty in Seoul. Elliott led his men overland some thirty miles through Korean territory rather than risk navigating the unknown Han River at night in the cruiser's steam launches. The Americans trekked through the countryside for eleven hours and arrived at the legation on the verge of collapse from the extreme heat and humidity. When the column entered Seoul, a uniformed Japanese horseman employed as a guide rode his mount at the head of the infantry. Crowds of Koreans attired in their traditional white garments and high black hats watched sullenly as the Americans paraded behind the proud Japanese rider. "This act," Sill wrote Day, "added intensity to a growing anti-American feeling." The Japanese guide knew the shortest route to the capital, Day replied, and "I don't care what nationality he is, and for his bad manners in riding his horse through the Legation gate I am in no way responsible, nor do I regard the fact that he did so a matter of political or any other consequence whatever." [55]

As the two officials bickered, the handful of weary men settled into the legation, and Sill expected them to keep the peace around the compound. Step by step diplomats dragged the United States into the East Asian dispute of 1894. A warship sent to Chemulpo, vague pledges to Korea, protests to Japan, and the landing of American soldiers promised to entangle the U.S. government in distant hostilities. Inspired by concerns of justice and humanity rather than self-interest, Gresham and Cleveland responded spontaneously to sudden demands to save missionaries and aid a pitiful and helpless little country. The two leaders felt morally and legally obligated to work for peace. "Acting under a stipulation in our treaty with Korea," the president advised Congress, "I felt constrained at the beginning of the controversy to tender our good offices to induce an amicable arrangement of the initial difficulty growing out of the Japanese demands for administrative reforms in Korea; but the unhappy precipitation of actual hostilities defeated this kindly purpose." [56]

Copyright 1903 by A. Loeffler. Reproduced by permission from the collection of the Library of Congress.

2

Neutrality

The Korean rebellion of 1894 introduced the Cleveland administration to East Asian problems. Unexpected requests for protection and pleas for diplomatic intervention forced the government to look beyond the Pacific Ocean, past Hawaii and Samoa, to remote China, Japan, and Korea. The antiexpansionist president and his secretary of state expressed little enthusiasm and less understanding of Asian diplomacy, but as outside pressures pulled their attention to the Far East, they did not hesitate to take the initial steps toward larger commitments in the area. Sending gunboats and landing marines might be an accepted approach to disturbances in Latin America, but it was another question to pursue this same conduct in Korea since the United States did not consider the peninsula vital to its security or a sphere of influence. American commerce in the kingdom remained insignificant, and though both Cleveland and Gresham desired the natural development of trade in the area neither actively promoted it. Yet the president ordered his minister to use every effort to keep the peace, while the secretary of state rushed a blunt note to a friendly power asking it to stay out of neighboring territory vital to its national interest, and fifty armed American men marched through a foreign land. Evidently other concerns moved the second Cleveland administration to interfere in East Asia. Gresham had previously revealed some of these motives in his Hawaiian and Korean policies. The United States as a democratic and antiimperialist power, he imagined, had moral obligations to preserve peace and stability in the world while upholding *de jure* governments against rebels or invaders who attempted to oust them illegally. He failed to realize that this moralistic and legalistic diplomacy often led to the same kinds of overseas complications and military interventions commonly attributed to expansionist and belligerent governments. Moreover, as Gresham soon discovered, an idealistic foreign policy limited flexibility and placed the United States at the mercy of distant events.

While Korean troubles remained localized, the chance of further entanglement appeared remote. China and Japan had settled earlier squabbles in 1884 through diplomacy, and fighting might still be avoided. The U.S. government did not expect a Sino-Japanese war, despite Tateno's boasts, and delayed dispatches from American representatives in Asia reinforced this opinion. Minister Denby's last report written just before he returned to the United States for an operation spoke of the tranquil and peaceful conditions in the Far East. The summer of 1894 would be exceptionally quiet, Denby assured the State Department, since China planned to celebrate the birthday of the venerable empress dowager.[1]

A series of reports from other diplomats in Eastern Asia reached Washington in late July and upset this complacency. The Chinese emperor seemed "hot for war," Sheridan P. Read wrote from his Tientsin consular post on July 22, and he advised his government to send a warship to the treaty port. The following day Consul General Thomas R. Jernigan cabled identical intelligence from Shanghai. War appeared inevitable, he observed, and the Chinese threatened to close the port to all foreign shipping. Minister Sill supported this view, since he had observed a large Japanese force march out of Seoul toward the Chinese army. Charles Denby Jr., substituting for his father, reported last on conditions in the troubled region. Japan's easy occupation of Seoul humiliated China, he informed Gresham, and "the Emperor and conservative statesmen are eager for war." [2]

Sino-Japanese warfare had, in fact, already started on the peninsula, but even those Americans in the immediate vicinity voiced uncertainty as to the extent of hostilities.

The Japanese had secured control of the country surrounding Seoul and had instituted military law, Captain Day revealed, but since telegraphic communications had been interrupted, he did not know whether China or Japan had declared war. Captain of Marines Elliott, closer to Sino-Japanese troops than any other American, also groped for information. "There is a rumor that war has actually and formally been declared between Japan and China," he observed on July 28, and "if this is true, our government will of course be in possession of the official information." [3]

The U.S. government had no information on the subject, official or otherwise. The Chinese and Japanese legations in Washington provided nothing in the way of war news, and the only intelligence reaching the capital during this interval of undeclared war came by delayed cables from its scattered diplomatic and naval agents in East Asia or from press releases originating in Shanghai and transmitted through the British-controlled cable. Communications required a month or more to reach the State Department and even then rested in some bureau as a clerk copied it, filed it, and then sent it on to the proper desk. Moreover, about this time each year government officials, including the president, left the moist, hot air of Washington for New England, many not returning until October. An important document followed them around for days and might not reach them in time for a decision. [4]

Gresham alone appeared concerned over the state of affairs in the Far East during the early summer of 1894, and he waited impatiently for news. Anxious to pursue a correct policy in the event of actual war, he telegraphed Colonel Denby for advice. The secretary asked Denby, then convalescing from his recent operation at the Cadillac Hotel in Detroit, whether he felt well enough to return to Peking. Aware of his old friend's pride and confidence in his son, Gresham tempered his remarks with praise for the young diplomat. "Your son will doubtless look after our interests in China about as well as you could," he assured the senior Denby, but the president has "indicated that he thought it would be well if you were there." [5]

Gresham's efforts to speed Denby back to his diplomatic post became more urgent when he learned about the *Kowshing* incident. This new trouble involved a 1,000-ton, steel, British built and registered steamship called *Kowshing*. This vessel shuttled Chinese troops and war supplies between China and Korea and on the evening of July 25, 1894, was intercepted by Japanese cruisers just off the peninsula. When the transport attempted to escape capture, the Japanese sent her to the bottom with the loss of over one thousand lives. As the Chinese infantry, European advisers, and British crew members abandoned ship, allegedly the Japanese gunners shot the survivors as they struggled in the water. Several dozen Chinese and a few Westerners, including German mercenary Colonel Constantin von Hanneken, escaped to tell the sensational story of the *Kowshing* massacre.[6]

The Japanese government expected a strong protest from the United States. They remembered Gresham's note delivered to Tokyo during the Korean crisis and wished to avoid similar expressions of diplomatic displeasure. Intent upon cultivating pro-Japanese sympathies in the United States, Japan launched a propaganda campaign in the American press designed to explain the motives behind *Kowshing*'s sinking. Foolish warmongers and fire-eaters did not determine policy, Japanese officials explained, but careful and mature statesmen guided Japan's destiny. Playing upon current fears of radicalism in the United States, these spokesmen insisted, "It would be just as fair to judge Japan's attitude at the present time by listening only to Japan's jingoes, as it would be to form an estimate of American statesmen from the examples afforded by Gen. Coxey and Mr. Debs."[7] Japanese consular agents stressed the theme of progressive Japan reforming backward Korea while the Tokyo government released a lengthy statement explaining its treaty obligations in Korea and China's efforts to obstruct them.[8]

Gresham and the U.S. government had no intention of responding to the incident, and though Americans discussed the *Kowshing* sinking, surprisingly few blamed the Japanese. The naval attack almost relieved the State Department of its uncertainty since it meant declarations of war by China and Japan on August 1, 1894. Weeks of confusion and indecision appeared over, and Gresham expected to formulate a neutral policy appropriate to a war between two nations friendly to the United States.[9]

China and Japan set out at once to preserve American friendship, or at least to assure neutrality. Under international law, a state of war required a neutral policy if the government was convinced that each belligerent had just cause for war.[10] Hence the two Asian nations endeavored to justify their position to the U.S. government. Japan would fight China "consistently with the law of nations," Japanese officials, trained in the subtleties of Western diplomacy, assured Washington. The tiny, five-man Japanese legation staff in the United States defended the decision for war. Miyaoka Tsunejiro, legation secretary and chargé d'affaires ad interim, explained Japan's justification to Secretary Gresham on August 1. China had forced Japan's declaration of war, he argued, by refusing to cooperate with her in reforming barbaric and decadent Korean institutions. Gresham, of course, had heard all this before, but Miyaoka added a new argument, claiming that China's pleas for Anglo-American mediation had been a ruse to buy time so that it could strengthen its military forces in Korea.[11]

China countered with its own interpretation of the war's background. The Chinese Foreign Office or Tsungli-yamen released a detailed summary of its Korean policies to Acting Minister Denby in Peking. At the same time former Chinese minister to the United States, Chang Yin-huan, outlined China's defense in a letter to Ambassador Bayard which he forwarded to Gresham. China could not, under the customs and laws of its tributary relation to Korea, enter a program of internal reform with Japan. When Bayard had been secretary of state in 1887, Chang noted, he had acknowledged Korea's tributary status. Japan had invaded Korea, Chang argued, while China had been invited in by the Korean government to suppress the Tonghak rebels. He also appealed to Bayard's moral sensitivities, citing Japan's unprovoked and savage attack on *Kowshing* during a time of peace as a flagrant violation of international law.[12]

Gresham felt both sides presented adequate cases for their war declarations, and since both expressed continued friendship the only correct policy must be strict neutrality. Ample precedents existed for neutrality during East Asian wars. The Pierce-Marcy administration had maintained American impartiality between China and Great Britain during the *Arrow* incident of 1856 despite violations by U.S. officials in Asia and pressures at home to join a Western alliance against China. President James Buchanan had continued and strengthened this policy when Anglo-French forces fought the Chinese between 1858 and 1860. "Our minister to China [John E. Ward], in obedience to his instructions," Buchanan had informed Congress in 1860, "has remained perfectly neutral in the war between Great Britain and France and the Chinese Empire." [13] Just a decade before the Sino-Japanese conflict, Secretary of State Frederick J. Frelinghuysen had further defined U.S. neutrality in the Franco-Chinese War. Now, in 1894, Gresham added his name to the list of nineteenth-century American statesmen who had defended the principles of neutrality in East Asia.

A neutral policy, Gresham soon discovered, brought with it diplomatic, legal, and moral complications. Controversial issues included the definition of contraband, blockade, and neutrality violations. Previous administrations had left some of these questions unanswered in their neutral relations with warring nations in the Far East. Chinese vessels had been sold to Americans during the Franco-Chinese War but the validity of such transactions had never been tested. At the same time, France had declared rice contraband though once again no opportunity had arisen to dispute the French claim.[14]

While unresolved principles troubled Gersham, nothing plagued him more than neutrality evasions by speculators, businessmen, and expansionists. Steamers on both coasts loaded war supplies for belligerent armies, much of it clearly contraband. Hawaiian annexationists, claiming that the United States faced eventual exclusion from world markets by victorious Asians, urged businessmen to exploit the Sino-Japanese conflict and achieve economic domination over Pacific Ocean and China markets before Asians could compete with them. Others interested in the extension of American influence in the area demanded repeal of any neutrality law which hindered expansion and the removal of all trade restrictions during the fighting. William Randolph Hearst, for one, goaded California munitions and shipbuilding firms to circumvent the neutrality proclamations of the "law-abiding administration." His editorials advised the Union Iron Works to construct fast torpedo boats and cruisers for Samoa but, once the warships put to sea, to turn them over to Japan.[15]

Some businessmen, though less sanguine than Hearst, predicted that the war would open East Asian markets to the United States. After Russell and Company had closed its Canton office in 1891, no American commercial house remained in China to promote trade, and commerce fell to its lowest point since the golden days of the late eighteenth and early nineteenth centuries when New England and New York merchants had competed with the English for domination of this lucrative marketplace. Perhaps the present controversy would revive this trade, and manufacturers asked the government to inform them of new commercial opportunities brought about by the Sino-Japanese War. At the same time, some predicted that continued fighting would stimulate American industry and alleviate unemployment and overproduction at home. Focusing on the current disagreement over silver and gold money in the United States, one writer added that at least the war would raise the price of silver and "not only help both our own Treasury and that of the Indian Government to unload part of the enormous quantity of silver bullion which they have accumulated, but may also render it possible to work at a profit our silver mines in the West that are now idle." [16]

The few labor commentators who discussed the war in

1894 agreed with business observers that the conflict bene-
fited not only the economy but also the workingman.
Though most wars exploited laboring people, these scribes
claimed, this struggle created jobs and an end to depression
in the United States. As the Knights of Labor publication
promised, the Asian war would eliminate competition from
cheap Oriental labor because "all the patriotic Japs and
Chinamen" would "go there now and be killed for glory
and relief of America." [17]

Not every American who wrote about the war during
the summer of 1894 assumed it would improve economic
conditions in the United States. Asian warfare, a few antiimperialists and pacifists contended, hindered the world's
economy by dislocating commerce, destroying property, and
creating hardship. Only war profiteers gained from the
fighting, and the United States had a duty to stop the war
since it had contributed to the hostilities through its reck-
less sale of arms to the Japanese and Chinese. The American Peace Society, for one, demanded that Washington
prevent any more weapons from reaching Asia.[18]

While the war served as a minor point of contention in
the long-running debate between antiimperialists and advocates of territorial acquisition, entrepreneurs busily
exploited the Asian situation. Ships loaded with flour,
beans, pork, beef, fruit, and leather goods destined for
hostile armies departed from San Francisco harbor. The
steamer *Rio de Janeiro* sailed with 200 tons of pig lead
consigned to Japan while the Armour Packing Company
of Kansas City negotiated with the belligerents for the sale
of 500,000 pounds of canned corn beef. A small Jersey City
company signed a contract to supply the Japanese army
with dried beef. Arms merchants remained active and Hart-
ley and Graham, New York agents for the Remington gun
works, sold several million rounds of ammunition to the
Japanese. The Charles R. Flint brokerage house allegedly
negotiated Japanese purchase of the Chilean cruiser *Esme-
ralda* through the Ecuadorean consul general in New York.
Cramps Shipbuilding of Philadelphia reportedly prepared
to sell the modern cruiser *Minneapolis* to the highest Asian

bidder, though it had already been contracted for the United States Navy. Marine insurance companies raised interest rates on war-risk goods and carried on a brisk trade. In fact, as one war speculator noted, "all lines of trade report an increased business, which is attributed to the Oriental War." [19]

Questionable activities during the war proved more attractive than legitimate enterprise. California gunrunners outfitted a swift merchantman to slip by patrolling cruisers used to enforce neutrality laws and to evade a Japanese blockade of the China coast. In China an American purchased the small steamers *Smith* and *Cass* to shuttle munitions under the American flag from mainland China to the island of Formosa. Captain G. W. Conner, an American officer working for the Japanese Steamship Company, continued to serve his foreign employers even when other neutral officers resigned. He remained with the company after it fitted out coastal vessels with quick-firing guns and ferried troops and supplies to Japanese front lines.[20]

Applications for service in the Japanese army from assorted military men, adventurers, and cranks flooded the Japanese legation in Washington, and officials issued a circular discouraging volunteers. Undeterred, ex-Confederate soldiers vied with Union counterparts to offer aid to Japan. Cecil Spring-Rice, a secretary at the British legation in the U.S. capital, remembered his conversation in August 1894 with one such enthusiastic Civil War veteran. "He is anxious to volunteer for the Japano-Chinese War," the Englishman wrote, "and was rather disappointed when I told him there was no chance of being accepted." [21] In Ohio several members of the local militia formed a Japanese Loyal Legion and received seventy signatures when they circulated enlistment forms for enrollment, while in California a recruiter organized a regiment for service in Asia and promised to equip prospective fighters with repeating rifles, special uniforms, and orders to loot rich mandarins' palaces. On the East Coast striking miners in Pennsylvania offered to enlist in the emperor's army. Interest in the war had reached such a point that when a cashier of the Second

National Bank of Altoona absconded with the contents of the safe, a newspaper reported his intention of donating the money to Japan's war fund.[22]

A sensational case of neutrality violation originated with the scheme of a New England inventor to build an infernal machine for China. The late Victorian imagination thrived on tales of sinister devices and awful engines of destruction. It was an age in which M. Eugene Turpin's engine of war thrilled Paris, General Clarke's secret electrical fish-shaped torpedo amazed Americans, and rumors of deadly balloon plots caused Londoners to shudder. John Wilde, a Rhode Island nautical inventor and sometime chemist, also had concocted a mysterious weapon which he claimed would destroy entire fleets without the loss of a single attacking ship. When Wilde offered his invention, a combination of chemically induced smoke screens and advanced torpedo boats, to the United States Navy, it ignored him. Now the aging, eccentric New Englander brooded in his waterfront laboratory, planning to show the world the power of his terrible secret.[23]

Wilde interested a George Cameron, alias George Howie, in his ideas. Cameron had been a demolitions expert during the Brazilian Revolution of 1893–1894 and more recently tested torpedoes for a local Rhode Island ordnance company. When news of possible Sino-Japanese hostilities reached Providence in early July 1894, Wilde wrote Japanese Minister Tateno and offered his invention to Japan. Wilde assured Tateno that he possessed secret information which Japan could use to destroy the entire Chinese navy. The Japanese official rejected his proposal. Wilde turned next for help to senior Rhode Island Senator Nelson W. Aldrich, well known for his efforts to expand American influence in East Asia and for his opposition to the narrow, legalistic foreign policies of the present administration. On August 27 Aldrich asked the Chinese minister to interview Wilde, who "desires to confer with you in regard to some matter which he will present." [24] The legation secretary and first interpreter, C. F. Moore, who had Anglicized his name and wore his pigtail under a wig, invited the men to his office. He expressed interest in the scheme and checked with former Secretary of State Foster, a dignified old gentleman with a special sympathy for China, to discover whether one of these men had served in the Brazilian Revolution. Foster inquired at Brazil's legation where Minister Salvador de Mendoza assured him that Brazil had employed an American explosives expert.[25]

Foster recommended acceptance of Wilde's offer, and Moore searched for funds to finance the expedition to China, but even the Chinese minister refused to contribute any money for this scheme. Wilde urged the interpreter to try harder. "If I get there before the war is over through your endeavors," he promised, "it will mean Rank, Honor and Wealth for you." [26] Somehow Wilde raised traveling expenses to San Francisco where he and Moore secured $6,000 from the local Chinese community. Joined by Cameron, the trio left the West Coast on October 16, 1894, bound for Tientsin aboard the mail steamer *Gaelic*. Once at sea, the adventure began to resemble a bad Gilded Age novel or stage play as Japanese agents shadowed the three and a drunken Cameron boasted of his ominous "machine-de-guerre" to a silent gentleman who turned out to be the Japanese consul in San Francisco.

Upon arriving in Yokohama, the plotters slipped ship and boarded the French steamer *Sydney* moored at the same wharf. The ruse failed, however, and when *Sydney* stopped at Kobe, Japanese marines surrounded her and arrested the three men. The patrol found a contract in Moore's pocket which outlined terms of sale and guaranteed destruction of the Japanese fleet. According to these documents, China had promised to pay the Americans one million dollars in gold and a percentage of every ship destroyed. This seemed amazing since a few days before the prisoners had struggled to raise a few dollars for steamship tickets. In any event, the Japanese Foreign Office examined the papers and forwarded the complete file to the American government.[27]

The so-called *Sydney* incident threatened to involve the United States in a controversy with Japan. Newspapers termed the arrest another Mason and Slidell case, in reference to the two Confederate agents seized on board a British ship during the American Civil War. They expected the U.S. government to demand immediate release of the prisoners. In Japan, American consul E. J. Smithers presented a vigorous protest to the captain of the Japanese warship *Tsukuba Kan* for intercepting *Sydney* and removing the three passengers. "No information having been received by me that martial law has been proclaimed by the Japanese government at this port," Smithers wrote from Hyogo, "I deem it my duty to protest and by this letter do hereby solemnly protest against the arrest and detention of the foresaid persons, holding you and whoever may be concerned responsible for the consequence of the said unlawful arrest and detention." [28]

Secretary Gresham, who considered the case an example of illegal activity on the part of greedy Americans, refused to support Smithers' complaint. He instructed Minister Dun to insure only that Japan treated the two white men properly as prisoners of war. The Japanese government responded to Gresham's calm, judicious approach by releasing Wilde and Cameron on their promise not to take up arms against Japan and to stay clear of Chinese territory. Though the Americans later broke their pledge and probably helped China fortify Weihaiwei, a potentially serious neutrality dispute had ended with a minimum of friction.[29]

The bizarre incident forced Washington to take precautions against further neutrality violations. Federal officers hunted the mysterious California recruiter, and government lawyers planned legal action against the Colt Arms factory in Hartford, Connecticut, at the request of the Japanese minister, who objected to the sale of ten million cartridges to China. Consul General Jernigan in Shanghai prevented shipment of arms to Formosa in *Cass* and *Smith,* both of which now flew the American flag. The Ecuadorean government, on Washington's command, suspended its consul general in New York until he answered charges that he had sold a Chilean cruiser to Japan. It was necessary further for the State Department to curb relief projects to feed starving Asians sponsored by American missionaries for fear that the food would fall into the hands of belligerent armies.[30] At the same time, Secretary Gresham initiated other precautionary measures. He instructed diplomats in East Asia to "issue all manner of writs to prevent the citizens of the United States from enlisting in the military or naval service of either of the said countries to make war upon any foreign power with whom the United States are at peace." The secretary gave ministers, consuls, and naval officers authority to use force, if necessary, to stop such neutrality violations.[31]

Japanese and Chinese threats to neutral rights and freedom of the seas posed another problem for Gresham. China announced plans to blockade the treaty ports of Amoy, Canton, Ningpo, Chinkiang, Foochow, Shanghai, Hankow, and Tientsin by removing buoys and channel markers and shutting down coastal lighthouses. Japan, meanwhile, planted mines at entrances to her own harbors. Similar conditions had existed during Franco-Chinese warfare a decade earlier when China had blocked Canton and Foochow harbors, but both Secretary Frelinghuysen and his successor Bayard had tolerated the inconvenience to shipping. Gresham also acquiesced, considering these war measures more a temporary nuisance than a threat to neutral rights.[32] Then on August 10 Chinese authorities at Shanghai announced arrangements to search American merchant vessels for war supplies. The secretary considered search and seizure far more dangerous than blockade, and he maintained regular communications with Acting Minister Denby. If China searched American merchantmen on the high seas, he wrote the young diplomat, "you will immediately report the fact for instructions, but you are not expected to encourage the assertion of that right." Under no circumstances, Gresham added, would the U.S. government permit the search of men-of-war or the disclosure of planned ship movements. However, since neither Japan nor China had stopped any American ship, he told the younger Denby, Washington expected to escape any threats to its maritime rights.[33]

The British, not China or Japan, posed the final menace

to U.S. neutrality. Britain pressed for American participation in proposed naval action against any nation which prevented free access to China's treaty ports. Sir Julian Pauncefote, the British minister in Washington, discussed the possibilities of allied cooperation in several meetings with Gresham. The secretary informed Sir Julian that the United States government would not compromise its policy of impartiality and friendship toward either belligerent, even to keep the ports open to Western commerce. The Cleveland administration, Gresham told reporters, would not participate in any joint intervention against China, Japan, or Korea. Ironically, the newspapers accused him of negotiating entangling alliances with European powers to keep the treaty ports free to foreign shipping. Nothing was further from the secretary's mind.[34]

Despite this most recent criticism and some embarrassing neutrality violations, Gresham pursued a policy of strict impartiality toward the two East Asian belligerents and initiated measures to preserve continued American amity toward China and Japan. His neutrality program during the Sino-Japanese War of 1894–1895 compared favorably to similar conduct by earlier secretaries of state during the Anglo-Chinese controversy of 1856 known as the *Arrow* affair, the Anglo-French-Chinese War several years later, and more recently during the Franco-Chinese War. Gresham's actions imitated earlier neutrality principles and hence did not create any major new problems in this particular diplomatic sphere. The secretary found the definition of policies during the war far easier than those required by the Hawaiian and Korean rebellions. But before long, fresh difficulties brought about by the extension of good offices to Japan and China destroyed the statesman's initial confidence.

3

Good Offices

Gresham did not expect any predicaments to arise from the extension of American good offices to China and Japan in 1894. It meant simply the offer of unofficial and impartial advice by a third party to two disputants, sometimes as the first step toward mediation. More often, though, it served as a useful channel of communications into and out of nations at war. Good offices was a humane policy and conformed to the highest standards of international law, two principles consistent with Gresham's conception of diplomacy. Adequate precedent existed for employing good offices to help settle Asian disputes. The United States had offered its services in the Russo-Japanese contest over the Sakhalin Islands in 1871, in the *Maria Luz* case between Peru and Japan in 1872, and most recently in the Franco-Chinese War of 1883–84. Clauses calling for American good offices could be found in treaties with Asian nations, particularly in Article I of the Korean-American Treaty of May 22, 1882. "If other powers deal unjustly or oppressively with either government," it read, "the other will exert their good offices, on being informed of the case, to bring about an amicable agreement, thus showing their friendly feeling." [1]

Gresham and Cleveland had employed Article I of the Korean-American covenant as the basis for interference in the peninsular rebellion of 1894, and though it had caused some trouble, they could not ignore similar pleas for good offices from Japan and China. Even before actual fighting, both nations inquired whether, in the event of a Sino-Japanese war, the United States would use its good offices to protect Japanese archives and subjects in China and those of China located in Japan. These requests received Washington's friendly response, and in late July 1894 Gresham forwarded ciphered telegrams to young Denby and Minister Dun instructing them to act as custodians of Chinese and Japanese interests in their respective posts. The secretary warned them not to extend official diplomatic representation to subjects of either Asian empire.[2]

Denby Jr. and Dun circulated Gresham's instructions to consular agents throughout China and Japan, but the directive confused everyone concerned, and diplomats asked for a further definition of their duties under good offices. Hoping to clarify his government's position, Acting Minister Denby distributed an ambiguous explanatory dispatch to consuls. American representatives would protect Japanese subjects in China but would not serve as officials of the Japanese government, he wrote. The consuls might become custodians of Japanese consulates and archives but could not fly the American flag over the buildings or act as Japanese consular agents. This explanation did not clarify the situation since at the same time the State Department told its consuls that the "raising of the flag of the United States over buildings owned or occupied in China by the Japanese Government would be perfectly proper and according to precedent." Though it later reversed this instruction, at the beginning of the war Washington clouded the application of custodial good offices in East Asia.[3]

The Japanese chargé d'affaires and his entire staff vacated Peking on August 1, leaving Americans in command of Japan's interests in China. Young Denby asked the Tsungliyamen to issue stringent orders to local authorities to protect Japanese subjects traveling from the interior to the treaty ports.[4] But tensions, misunderstandings, and confrontations brought about by the extension of protection to belligerents could not be avoided. On August 2 Consul Read, in accordance with his instructions, escorted the Japanese consul's family through hostile, shouting Chinese mobs to a British steamer waiting to take them home to Japan. Read placed them aboard ship and returned to his

Tientsin consulate, but as soon as he had departed, Chinese soldiers and ruffians rushed the British vessel and removed every Japanese passenger. They bound the consul's wife and tossed her out on the wharf. Read intervened at once and requested provincial governor Li Hung-chang, one of China's most powerful bureaucrats, to reprimand the soldiers and allow Japanese to return to the ship. The aged commander of China's northern defenses complied and released the Japanese, but the incident increased anti-Western feeling at the treaty port.[5]

Consul General Jernigan at Shanghai reported other problems arising from good offices. The department's instructions "so disquieted Americans that I was pressed to communicate with you," Jernigan announced, "submitting that the course of the United States toward China and Japan be absolutely neutral in the interest of American interests in both countries." He suspected that the service would destroy Sino-American friendship and "would tend to transfer to American residents in China the intense animosity of the Chinese for Japanese and especially endanger the lives of American missionaries in the interior of this Empire." [6]

Although less critical than the Chinese situation, custodial good offices also caused difficulties in Japan. When a Japanese mob stoned some Chinese, N. W. McIvor, the American consul general at Kanagawa, provided protection for 500 persons making their way to the docks to board the China-bound steamship *Oceanic*.[7] Another annoyance stemmed from Chinese assertions that the United States held diplomatic and legal jurisdiction over them as long as they resided in Japan. The State Department denied this, but nevertheless good offices obscured the line where American authority terminated and Japanese responsibilities began. The Japanese government issued an ordinance, proclaiming that its courts and not U.S. consuls had control over Chinese subjects in Japan. McIvor tried to appease local officials and explained that the United States had not chosen sides in the war but acted as "a friend of good order and civilization" in East Asia.[8] Japan, increasingly sensitive to her treaty rights and buoyed by her military victories, seemed satisfied by McIvor's explanation and caused no further problems for American representatives trying to perform their duty under the broad application of good offices.

Up to this point, the Cleveland administration had suffered only minor embarrassment from its wartime diplomacy. It remained unprepared for the question of Japanese spies in China, however. For years the Japanese intelligence service had infiltrated China with agents disguised as students, merchants, and even missionaries. They supplied the Japanese army with detailed maps of the countryside and sketches and elaborate descriptions of major fortifications and arsenals. The Chinese obtained some knowledge of this network and with the declaration of war announced severe punishment for any Japanese captured as a military spy. They suspected every Japanese citizen in China, and this, combined with American protection of Japanese in the Chinese Empire, led to a volatile situation. Charles Denby Jr. tried to avoid a confrontation by urging the Chinese to "proceed with moderation and to be influenced rather by motives of humanity than by bitterness toward Japan." He asked the Peking government to deport not execute suspected spies.[9]

With the outbreak of hostilities, Japanese citizens in China flocked to the treaty ports in preparation for their voyage to Japan. At Shanghai, Jernigan promised protection to local Japanese if they decided to remain at the coastal city. The first test of Jernigan's pledge occurred on August 10 when two Japanese students accused of spying requested asylum in the American consulate. The consul general welcomed them, offered sanctuary, and refused demands for their surrender to Chinese authorities. The Tsungli-yamen protested and instructed Yang Ju to press the United States government on the issue.[10] Yang's remonstrance surprised Gresham, and he cabled Acting Minister Denby to "report immediately and fully" on China's complaint. "Our legation and consulates in China," he warned, "are not authorized to hold Japanese accused of crime against the demand of Chinese authorities." [11]

Denby Jr. confirmed Yang's report but defended Jernigan's action. The two Japanese students had been arrested by the French consul in Shanghai's International Settlement, were under extraterritorial jurisdiction, and legally must be tried by consular agents and not by Chinese bureaucrats. Moreover, the pair had requested asylum in the American compound under good offices, and Jernigan had granted this fully in accord with Gresham's instructions to protect all Japanese in China. Denby Jr. wondered if the secretary now contradicted this policy.[12]

All his life, Gresham had separated controversial questions into categories of right and wrong, legalities and illegal acts, and this case seemed no different. Jernigan and Denby Jr. behaved illegally by harboring these accused criminals from the proper authorities and operated unconstitutionally by affording official representation to the citizens of another nation. Their conduct toward the two Japanese showed special favor to one side and contradicted the laws of strict neutrality. "You and Consul General at Shanghai seem to misapprehend nature of protection authorized," Gresham cabled Denby Jr. "Lending good offices does not invest Japanese with extraterritoriality nor should legation or consulates be made asylum for Japanese who violate local laws or commit belligerent acts." Jernigan should not give fugitives refuge and was not authorized to protect them any longer.[13]

Colonel Denby's son refused to yield and, unable to convince Gresham on legal grounds, turned next to moral suasion. The surrender of the two alleged spies, termed "mere schoolboys, peacefully and openly living in Shanghai," meant terrible torture and decapitation by barbaric Chinese. He begged Gresham to delay this unconditional surrender to the Chinese government until his father returned to Peking.[14] The secretary replied curtly, "My instructions 29th clear." [15] Denby Jr. instructed Jernigan to hand the two students over to Chinese authorities, but the young diplomat was not finished with Gresham and expended his anger by sending an elaborate and condescending explanation of Western law in China to the secretary of state. The foreign concession in Shanghai required a multiple legal code, he argued, and mixed courts with a Chinese magistrate and a foreign assessor tried cases in the international community. Gresham not only misunderstood this but threatened to undermine the entire treaty system and set a dangerous precedent for the future viability of extraterritoriality in the Far East.[16]

Denby did not tell his superior the real reason for his concern. Gresham's actions endangered the secure little Western enclave in Shanghai, where Americans and Europeans lived in an island of splendor separated from China's teeming humanity only by a thin brick wall. They resided in fine homes attended by scores of Oriental servants and played in the clubs, tennis courts, race tracks, and theaters of the Western section. The decaying remnants of Imperial China existed just outside the compound. Mud huts of impoverished peasants, opium dens with corrupt Manchu bureaucrats, and sweating coolies unloading cargoes from Western ships dominated late nineteenth-century Shanghai. Chinese entered the foreign settlement only as servants or to conclude business with some Western merchant. Foreigners carefully guarded this privilege and allowed nothing to upset this proper relationship. But Gresham's decision would open a rift in the glorious seclusion and immunity from actual conditions in China by permitting Chinese officials to enter the sanctuary and carry off two foreigners from the secure compound. In Asian terms, the Western community would lose face and the foreign settlement would seem less awesome. The acting minister did not reveal these forebodings to the secretary.[17]

While the Shanghai incident consumed most of the State Department's energy, good offices troubled Americans in other parts of China. At Hankow far up the winding Yangtze River, Consul Jacob T. Child relied on a "display of rifles" to protect Japanese subjects in that treaty port,[18] while at Tientsin near the Chinese capital Consul Read became involved in a controversy over the capture of an accused spy named Ishikawa Yoichi. Read believed the prisoner was an agent of the Japanese army, but Japan claimed he was not and fully expected the consul to use good offices to obtain his release.[19] In both cities the amicable service compromised American neutrality and further endangered lives. In fact, the Chinese accused American consular agents of arranging for the escape of spies and called the diplomats "dishonorable." [20]

A similar problem developed in Ningpo, just south of Shanghai. The Chinese seized a Japanese religious pilgrim at this port city and without evidence sentenced him to death for spying. The American consul, John Fowler of Boston, denounced the Chinese action and asked Peking for permission to save the condemned man. "Gresham's orders positive," Denby Jr. wrote from the capital; "consuls cannot protect Japanese accused of crime." The acting minister added, "You may use friendly offices to secure trial, if refused, no alternative." [21] This order angered Fowler, an exponent of increased American influence in China and a comrade of antiadministration critic, Massachusetts Senator Henry Cabot Lodge. Fowler may have expressed his frustrations to Lodge, because the senator later attacked Gresham's handling of custodial good offices.

The difficulties with good offices at other treaty ports increased interest in the Shanghai matter. The case of the two Japanese students became a sensitive issue in the State Department and in the press. Gresham had not consulted Third Assistant Secretary of State Rockhill, the department's Asian expert, and Rockhill expressed displeasure with his chief's narrowly conceived and ill-informed decision.[22] At the same time newspapers began to comment on the spy case, and leading editorials condemned Gresham's surrender to the Chinese. "The pledge of the United States to protect Japanese subjects in China is a mockery," one writer declared, "and should be at once withdrawn, so that Japan may be able to secure the good offices of some other power." [23]

Aging Consul General Jernigan, suffering from the extreme Shanghai heat, felt betrayed by Gresham's order. As one of Rockhill's friends wrote from China, Jernigan had "the Japanese spies on the brain and can talk of nothing else; and not with much dignity he inspires or writes himself articles belauding his own actions and belittling that of the State Department." [24] On September 21, Jernigan presented the department with a lengthy manuscript justifying his actions. He had protected the Japanese because of the excited state of the Chinese mind, Jernigan wrote, which would have meant death to the young men within a few hours. Gresham misunderstood conditions in China, and his instructions condemned the pair to death and endangered other Japanese citizens in China. "Viewed from a legal standpoint, the case presented no difficulty," the consul general concluded, "but I had been instructed to protect Japanese interests and here was a case that appeared, not to law, but to humanity. I was not asked to intervene legally, officially, but as a man having the confidence of both China and Japan, and desirous of being just to both and at least humane to the imperilled subjects of the one whose interest I have been published as being the representative at this port." [25]

Gresham adjudged his position correct; besides, Yang Ju assured him that the two students would not be punished until Colonel Denby returned to his ministerial post in Peking. "Reports in the American papers to the effect that the two alleged spies had been beheaded by the Chinese Government," Yang insisted, "were untrue." [26] Even Jernigan admitted as much and sent a cablegram to the department on October 9 to "belie newspaper reports" about the death of the pair. But two weeks later Jernigan reported the torture and decapitation of the two accused students.[27] Gresham considered the case closed.

During the latter part of November, Julian Ralph, a correspondent for *Harper's Weekly,* resurrected the issue. Looking for sensational copy, Ralph interviewed the guilt-ridden consul general in Shanghai. Freely interpreting many of Jernigan's comments, Ralph penned an article for *Harper's* which disclosed the whole tragic and sordid story.

The Japanese, Ralph wrote, had been "tortured with horrible ingenuity and devilishness, every day with new brutality, for seven days," and American helplessness had condemned them to this awful death. Embellishing on Jernigan's suspicions, the journalist blamed the "oily rogue" of a Chinese minister in Washington for blinding Gresham to reality and making him commit what almost amounted to murder.[28] The scurrilous article appeared in publications throughout the country, and Ralph believed that the U.S. Senate decided to investigate Gresham's conduct as a result of his revelations. On the very day that Ralph's essay appeared, Theodore Roosevelt wrote Henry Cabot Lodge about the affair and urged Lodge to demand all official correspondence concerning the case for a Senate inquiry. "It seems to me that this brutal stupidity and cowardice of Gresham in the matter of the surrender of the two Japanese calls for the most decided and prompt action," the future president told Lodge on December 1, 1894. "If possible I wish he could be impeached." [29]

Roosevelt saw Gresham's alleged cowardly act as a weakness unbecoming an American statesman, and Lodge viewed it as an opportunity to castigate the administration's foreign policies and increase his own stature in the Republican Party. Expansionists in the capital still resented Gresham's defeat of Hawaiian annexation, and this new issue provided Lodge and other imperialist senators with an ideal forum to discredit everything Gresham stood for. The vindictive Massachusetts senator began his attack on December 3 and demanded that the secretary turn over all relevant documents to the Senate.[30]

Gresham resisted this pressure and called Senator John T. Morgan of Alabama, chairman of the Foreign Affairs Committee, to his office to present the administration's position. Morgan, no friend of Gresham's diplomacy, personally disliked the secretary. The southern legislator advocated a high protective tariff, Hawaiian annexation, and American expansion. He had almost come to blows with Gresham in a previous meeting and the room had to be cleared to avoid a fight.[31] But this time Morgan listened

to Gresham's explanation of the spy case and agreed to
bring a ranking Republican back to read the secret correspondence in private to determine whether the whole Senate
should see it. Morgan, accompanied by Senator John
Sherman of Ohio, returned and discussed the case with
the secretary.

Gresham, not noted for his tact, could be blunt—some
said rude—and once he made up his mind often refused to
listen to contrary arguments, but in his meeting with Morgan and Sherman, Gresham presented a judicious and calm
defense of his conduct. The State Department could not
release the spy-case dispatches, he explained, because
public scrutiny of the documents endangered delicate treaty
negotiations now about to be concluded between the United
States and China. "There are some things in the correspondence the publication of which might irritate China, perhaps offend her," Gresham told the senators.[32] The secretary
convinced the two senior lawmakers to resist Lodge's untimely demands for documents, and on December 5 Sherman asked his colleagues to refer the matter to committee
rather than debate it on the Senate floor.

Lodge rejected Sherman's suggestion and launched a
tirade against the Cleveland-Gresham foreign policies. The
failure to protect the two young Japanese, Lodge argued,
was "an act of the greatest possible discredit to the humanity
of the United States and to the humanity of civilized men."
They had relied on American good offices but had been
betrayed and turned over to what Lodge called the most
hideous tortures. The people deserved an explanation for
such an incident, the Massachusetts senator insisted. Morgan defended the administration. "War is flagrant between
Japan and China," he retorted, "and the least interference
on the part of the Senate of the United States which might
be considered as favoring the one side or the other of those
belligerents would be an unfortunate circumstance at this
particular time." Pressed to explain why he thought the
documents on the affair should not be made public, Morgan
warned that imputations of guilt against the president, the

secretary of state, or American diplomatic agents ought to be studied before being debated in public.[33]

Lodge wavered. His resolution called simply for the facts and did not intend to disturb American relations with China and Japan. Then the Republican lawmaker fired a parting shot at the administration. He traced Washington's diplomacy during the Sino-Japanese War from its allegedly mischievous and meddling conduct during the Korean rebellion to its humiliating and disgraceful action in Shanghai. Cleveland and Gresham had already upset the U.S. position in East Asia, Lodge contended, and the public should be apprised of the disgraceful behavior. "If it be true that we gave up these men to torture and to death without a single inquiry after we had an understanding with the Chinese Government that we should give safe conduct to just such citizens in order to get them out of that country," he concluded, "then a heavy burden of misdoing rests on somebody." [34] Despite Lodge's pleas, though, Sherman's motion to defer the question to committee passed and the Senate recessed for the Christmas holiday.

Gresham wrote Colonel Denby, at last in Peking, about the Senate debate. When Congress reconvened, he told Denby, some of the dispatches written by the minister's son would be seized by the opposition to damage the government. Gresham blamed the trouble on Jernigan and not young Denby since controversy would have been averted if the consul general had followed Washington's instructions. "I do not expect any real trouble to come from the matter, however," he assured Denby, "and hope you will not let it annoy you." [35]

Even so, the Shanghai incident continued to bother Gresham, weakening his already poor health and increasing his irascibility. The secretary turned on Yang Ju for what he believed was the Chinese minister's betrayal of trust in promising that the Chinese government would wait for Denby's return before punishing the two alleged spies. "I regret to say that there is reason to believe that the men were executed before the return of Colonel Denby to Peking," Gresham complained to Yang, "and therefore, in derogation of the voluntary promise which you assured me your Government had made." [36] In his reply to the secretary, Yang insisted that Gresham had misunderstood their conversation since he had stated only that his government would take the matter under consideration. "It was established by proof that [the two students] had furnished information to their Government by means of ciphers in which seventy-six telegraphic messages in all were sent by them, giving reports of the movement of troops and of military matters." [37] Chinese officials could not wait for the American minister's return to dispense justice. Gresham pressed the issue in further correspondence, but Yang refused to argue, assuring the secretary that their differences remained merely a regrettable misunderstanding.[38]

The constant contention disturbed Gresham. Certain of his righteous position in the spy case, he deplored Ralph's innuendo, Lodge's demagoguery, and Jernigan's insubordination. He wanted the public to hear his interpretation of the story and compiled an unsigned defense for the *New York Evening Post,* a paper sympathetic with the Cleveland government. The *Post* defended Gresham and termed the criticism groundless and sensational. Other proadministration and independent newspapers also presented editorials favorable to Gresham, often noting that even the Japanese government admitted the United States could not legally prevent the execution.[39]

Republican editors countered these arguments with their own conception of administration conduct and attacked the supposed weak and vacillating policies of the current government. They claimed Gresham did not have a shred of evidence showing that the two boys were spies and everyone, even Colonel Denby, believed them innocent of clandestine activity. The cowardly secretary had surrendered harmless students under American protection to the bloodthirsty Chinese executioner. No sane leader would have acted in this manner, Whitelaw Reid suggested and wondered, "Is Gresham in his right mind?" [40]

Ironically Denby now supplied evidence that at least one

of the two victims had served the elaborate spy network
in China. The minister had gathered information about the
training and procedure of Japanese espionage agents and
noted that at one time thirty spies worked in Shanghai
alone. "I have it on the best authority," he asserted, "that
one of the alleged Japanese spies who was arrested at
Shanghai, and over whose fate so many tears have been
shed, was one of these detailed officers." Every village in
the projected war zone had been infiltrated by these scouts
disguised as storekeepers, monks, laborers, merchants, and
students. "This information, I think you will agree with
me, tends greatly to show that a vast amount of undeserved
sympathy has been wasted on Japanese spies, both in our
own country and in this." [41] Even Jernigan concurred and
informed Assistant Secretary of State Uhl that if allowed
to try the case he would have committed one and freed
the other.[42]

These revelations reinforced Gresham's determination to
continue the good offices policy. Its legality had never been
in doubt and Denby's latest report demonstrated its equity.
The United States government now employed good offices
to register Japanese citizens residing in China and those of
China living in Japan. The same service lay behind discussions of immunity from attack of unarmed belligerent
vessels, such as lighthouse boats. And finally, American
diplomats working under the auspices of good offices opened
channels of communication between Japan and China,
leading to peace negotiations. None of these functions,
though, perplexed the administration as much as the custodial aspects of the policy, but all meant increased involvement in East Asian affairs. An idealistic and well-meaning
policy had once again threatened American impartiality
and friendship. The Chinese resented good offices, and the
service endangered Americans as they attempted to protect
Japanese interests and as they mixed in domestic politics.
This in turn necessitated increased military forces in the
Far East and further entangled the U.S. government in a
remote war. Gresham's legalistic approach to the Sino-
Japanese War now led to gunboat diplomacy.

18. United States Gunboat Monocacy on the Pei-ho River. Tientsin, China. Copyright 1902 by C. H. Graves.

Copyright 1902 by C. H. Graves. Reproduced by permission from the collection of the Library of Congress.

4

Gunboat Diplomacy

Defense of Japanese interests in China stirred up antiforeign feelings and increased dangers faced by the nearly one
thousand American missionaries and their families in China.
These religious workers expected to be the main target of
Chinese reprisals against American assistance to the hated
Japanese "dwarf men." In 1894 several hundred Presbyterian, Methodist, and American Board of Commissioners
for Foreign Missions personnel resided in northern China
and constituted the single largest group of Americans in
the region closest to hostilities. These scattered bands of
missionaries had established chapels, schools, and dispen-
saries at remote stations in the interior. The majority la-
bored long hours, learned the native language, and lived
with the peasants. They coped with diseases which deci-
mated countless missionary families and with the distrust
and hostility of the people and officials. Anti-Western riots
had plagued China before, and Christian teachers often
faced death at the hands of Chinese mobs.

President Cleveland's major objective during the Sino-
Japanese War remained the protection of missionaries,
while he left Secretary Gresham in charge of other details
of the administration's response to East Asian relations in
1894 and early 1895. Concern for the lives of religious visitors forced the president to dispatch a warship to Chemulpo
and marines to Seoul during the Korean insurrection. Both
Cleveland and Gresham considered the presence of an
American man-of-war essential for the restoration of peace
and stability on the peninsula, and though they objected
to an aggressive and imperialist foreign policy, neither

opposed the use of force to prevent foreign or domestic rebellions and violence. They had previously indicated a willingness to employ gunboat diplomacy during the Brazilian Revolution and had rushed several warships to the Bay of Rio de Janeiro in early 1894. But the Asian disorders still seemed too remote to require more than one cruiser, and at first the Cleveland government hesitated to reinforce *Baltimore*. Provocation caused by good offices and the increased tempo of fighting, however, convinced Gresham and Cleveland that Americans in China faced greater dangers than those in Korea.

News from China in early August added to Washington's apprehension. First the administration learned that Manchu soldiers had slain a British missionary named James Wylie. Japanese victories, American diplomats in Peking and Tientsin warned the State Department, had turned Chinese against all foreigners, and lawless and demoralized infantry had insulted several U.S. citizens. "Much anxiety is felt among the foreigners at Tientsin for their own safety," Acting Minister Denby reported, and "if the Japanese land and defeat the Chinese, the routed soldiers will, it is feared, attack the settlement." [1]

Learning of Wylie's murder, missionaries urged the government to save them. American Board workers wrote numerous letters to their director, Judson Smith, in Boston, revealing deep concern for their safety. Chinese soldiery had become a destructive mob without discipline, Franklin M. Chapin observed from his Linching station, and medical missionary Willis C. Noble reported unrest at Paotingfu. Antiforeign rabble tormented Christians at this important American Board outpost, and Noble feared for his life and for the lives of the women in his party. Even missionaries residing in the treaty ports where Western gunboats and marines stood readily available expressed alarm. [2]

Aggressive church organizations in the United States pressed the administration to defend their agents in the Far East. "There is much reason to fear for the safety of the missionaries both men and women now stationed in China and Corea," Southern Methodist Bishop Alpheus

W. Wilson warned, and he sent a list of Methodist emis-
saries to the State Department. The executive committee of
foreign missions for the Southern Presbyterian Church
joined its Methodist brethren in petitioning Washington for
protection of its overseas apostles. The government should
take all necessary steps to safeguard its fifty missionaries
in China, the committee insisted, and it resolved to present
its case in person, dispatching the Reverend Dr. J. W.
Bachman to a Washington conference with Secretary of
State Gresham. Leaders of the Board of Missions of the
Northern Presbyterian Church in New York followed
Bachman to the capital and arranged their own meeting
with Gresham. The State Department in fact received many
letters from missionary groups and individuals having
friends and relatives in Asian missions.[3]

Gresham calmed their anxieties and assured religious
spokesmen that American missionaries faced no immediate
danger and would receive necessary protection. Privately,
though, he doubted whether the limited forces available
provided security.[4] He looked down the hall to the Navy
Department for help where sixty-year-old Hilary A. Herbert
busily reorganized the department and drew up plans for a
modern battleship navy along the lines advocated by Rear
Admiral Stephen B. Luce and Captain Alfred Thayer
Mahan. These gentlemen criticized the post-Civil War strategy of coastal defense and commerce raiding and proposed
the creation of a powerful battleship fleet to rival leading
naval powers of the world. But this new navy progressed very
slowly, and Herbert hoped to find a way to pry additional
funds for warships from a reluctant Congress. Thus when
Gresham rushed in with his complaints of inadequate naval
forces for East Asia, Herbert saw an opportunity to use the
Sino-Japanese War to press the legislature for more money.

Gresham, of course, did not have battleships in mind,
and as he told the president, the Sino-Japanese War required
"some small ships, able to run up the rivers" of China.[5]
Even this humble request provided an opportunity for
increased naval activity, and Herbert ordered available
cruisers and gunboats to the Far East. The 230-foot, 1,710-

ton gunboat *Concord,* completed in 1891, and the 176-foot, 892-ton *Petrel,* commissioned in 1889, sailed nearby in the Bering Sea watching the seals. Herbert dispatched these two tiny warships to China's waters. The more formidable 3,730-ton cruiser *Charleston,* built by Union Iron Works of San Francisco in 1889, rested at Mare Island Naval Yard undergoing repairs. The speedy cruiser, armed with six- and eight-inch breech-loading rifles and manned by 20 officers and 280 men, provided an ideal support ship for *Baltimore,* and Herbert ordered its commanding officer, Captain George W. Coffin, to get under way for China as soon as possible. The secretary also sent *Concord*'s sister ship *Yorktown,* as well as the 2,074-ton cruiser *Detroit,* noted for its intervention in the Brazilian Revolution of 1893–1894, and the 1,777-ton gunboat *Machias,* completed at the Bath Iron Works in Maine just the previous year, to the Asiatic Station.[6]

Secretary Herbert assigned command of the reinforced squadron to Rear Admiral Charles C. Carpenter, a massive man with thick mustache and wavy beard. Carpenter had served on the Asian patrol in 1884 where he had suffered the first in a series of physical and mental breakdowns. Though the senior officer committed suicide in a Massachusetts sanitarium several years after the Sino-Japanese War, in August of 1894 the department considered the experienced sailor capable of directing fleet operation in a critical area.[7] By late autumn Carpenter had two modern cruisers and four gunboats in East Asian waters and expected two more warships any day. These additions increased the flag officer's ability to respond to missionary requests for naval protection, but he realized that even the larger squadron provided inadequate strength to cover the scattered groups, protect Sino-Japanese interests under good offices, observe belligerent ship movements, and collect intelligence.

Carpenter devised a twofold strategy to derive maximum effectiveness from his ships. First, he deployed several vessels at what the Navy Department considered sensitive trouble spots, and he used the rest to maintain continual patrols around the war zone. Second, the officer cooperated with European naval commanders. While the State Department hesitated to join European powers in diplomatic ventures during the Sino-Japanese War, the Navy Department held no such reservations, and Secretary Herbert accepted the traditional policy of using European military cooperation to further American interests in the Far East.[8] The tough Civil War veteran suffered none of the moral reservations or idealistic concepts of international affairs which haunted Gresham. In any event, the U.S. had derived benefits before by tying itself to the British navy, and once again the British Asiatic fleet with nineteen trim fighting ships under the command of Vice Admiral E. R. Fremantle presented such an opportunity. Carpenter met Fremantle on November 4, and the English officer pledged cooperation with the U.S. Navy. He warned, however, that this arrangement constituted only an informal expression of mutual interest and did not guarantee joint naval maneuvers. Several days later Carpenter reached similar understandings with French and German naval officers in charge of their country's forces in East Asian waters.[9]

Joint European-American naval action never materialized, and United States naval officers pursued an independent, if somewhat primitive, brand of gunboat diplomacy in the Far East during the Sino-Japanese War. The most important patrol centered on the Gulf of Chihli which, bordered by the Liaotung Peninsula and Port Arthur to the north, Weihaiwei and Chefoo at the tip of the Shantung Peninsula to the south, and Tientsin and the Taku forts to the west, lay nearest the scene of fighting. Carpenter assigned responsibility for this station to *Charleston* and *Yorktown*. Though he occasionally joined the patrol, Carpenter preferred to maintain his flagship *Baltimore* at Nagasaki as a communications center rather than toss about on the rough winter seas.

The tiny *Yorktown* under the command of William Mayhew Folger responded to every missionary plea for assistance. The commander kept his crew drilled in landing and rescue operations, though he refused to put his men ashore even to save missionary lives. He also declined to intervene in local politics, despite the pleadings of long-time China resident Calvin Mateer. The American missionary begged Folger to ask Japanese naval officers to stop bombardment of the port city of T'ung-chou where Mateer and other Western religious representatives lived. "A state of war exists," the commander informed Mateer, "and, legally all foreigners that remain in the country do so at their own risk." [10] He offered to transport the Westerners to safety but no more. Mateer ignored Folger's advice and made repeated efforts to enlist the U.S. Navy as an intermediary between the missionary community and the Japanese command, offering even to surrender T'ung-chou if it would mean less bloodshed.[11]

Yorktown and *Charleston* chased after missionaries for several months, and more than once both narrowly missed running aground while waiting for religious workers who failed to appear on the coast as promised.[12] "As a class the missionaries are thoroughly helpless and irresponsible as far as taking precautions are concerned," Carpenter wrote Washington, "and by their lack of unanimity of action would defeat the best laid plans for their rescue." [13] He ordered missionaries to gather at Chefoo where his gunboats could protect them, but despite Carpenter's petition most remained in the surrounding countryside and seemed to expect protection in their own interior stations.

The Gulf of Chihli patrol exemplified the administration's ideal of protecting American lives without involvement on the Asian mainland. Unfortunately Gresham could not always communicate this larger policy to individual diplomats and naval officers. Minister Sill in Korea proved truculent and insisted upon keeping American soldiers on Korean territory, building winter barracks for them in his legation courtyard. "I have taken it for granted that the Navy Department will supply stoves and fuel and fit it up with bunks and blankets," Sill cabled Carpenter. The officer sent supplies but also reduced the size of the legation guard.[14] Several weeks later he asked Sill if all the men might be withdrawn. Sill replied that while the Chinese no longer threatened Seoul the whole kingdom appeared on the brink of anarchy and he recommended retention of some armed men. Though the minister feared for the lives of the eighty Americans around the Korean capital, he also became interested in U.S. participation in postwar reconstruction of Korea and in checking Japanese expansion on the peninsula. These troops would be useful for this purpose and should remain in Korea, not so much for protection against any immediate danger but because other Western powers left guards in the capital.[15]

Sill endeavored to convince Gresham of the need for an active Korean policy, and he dashed off a cable to the skeptical secretary informing him that troops prevented plots and assassination attempts. Again in December 1894 Sill wrote his chief about the failure of Japanese reforms which left Korea in complete disorder. The minister also reminded Washington of Korea's economic potential and revealed Japanese plans to open and develop the rich gold mines of the country. He wanted the United States to share this wealth.[16] Secretary Gresham, though, expected American ships and men to protect missionaries and assist in the good offices policy, not promote economic imperialism. He suspected Sill of heading in the direction of Minister Stevens and the corrupt sugar speculators who had entangled the United States in Hawaiian annexation controversies. Gresham ordered Sill's guard removed as soon as the European legation sentries returned to their ships. But Sill resisted this directive and informed Gresham, "In this city American citizens outnumber all other Caucasian nationalities combined and these are largely women and children. My responsibilities are greater than those of any European Representative, hence I cannot consent to follow blindly any example of withdrawal of guards that any of them may set." [17]

Meanwhile Sill's detachment had become an embarrassment to the United States government, though it provided the only excitement experienced in Seoul's otherwise secure foreign community. Several letters from sensitive American missionaries in Korea which accused U.S. soldiers of drunken debauchery reached Washington. One note charged inebriated marines with neglect of guard duty while another alleged the outrage of a Korean woman only recently converted to Christianity. "We have to blush for our American soldiers and some of the officers from the *Baltimore*," one missionary wrote. "They get beastly drunk and carouse about the streets in a most disgraceful manner, frightening and surprising the Japs and Koreans." [18]

Assistant Secretary of the Navy McAdoo ordered a complete investigation of military conduct in Korea and directed Carpenter and Captain Day to question the officers and crew of *Baltimore*. Embarrassed by the scandal, Minister Sill worked hard to allay suspicions. He found the source of the story, a busy female missionary prone to idle gossip, and passed this evidence on to Day. The officer cleared his men of wrongdoing and negligence of duty. "It would have been surprising, and not in accordance with the usual experience with landing parties had there not been some drunkenness amongst them as they were supplied with money monthly," Day reported. He admitted to navy veteran Carpenter, "Men who do not get drunk are not plentiful in the Navy and Marine Corps." The Navy Department dropped the investigation.[19]

Americans carried on a clumsy gunboat diplomacy at other East Asian stations. Similar situations occurred at Newchwang, Peking, and on the Yangtze River patrol which soon overshadowed the Korean episode. Newchwang, an important trading center at the mouth of the Liao River in northern China, reeked of stagnant water and filth. But the port housed a number of Westerners, and in early autumn 1894 the Navy Department dispatched the gunboat *Petrel* to the city but then changed its mind and canceled sailing orders. The departmental cable arrived too late to help the small warship which had already entered the harbor and become inextricably mired in the mud, trapping 10 officers and 122 men. The 892-ton gunboat remained disabled until spring rains could refloat her. The United States Navy did not have enough warships in the first place, and to lose another in the thick slime of Newchwang was most humiliating. The officers and crew made the best of this

ignominious situation by building a mud palisade around
the ship and mounting Gatling guns on the parapets. At
least one incident between a crew member and a Chinese
mob threatened for a time to erupt in violence, but *Petrel*
survived unharmed and actually served as a base for watching the movements of the Chinese army which daily passed
close to the stranded vessel.[20]

Concord, patrolling the Yangtze River, also invited
trouble. In one compromising predicament after another,
the gunboat blundered up and down the winding river. First,
commanding officer Caspar F. Goodrich, later president of
the United States Naval Institute at Annapolis, ignored
neutrality proclamations and forced a number of Chinese
gun sampans away from the landing pontoon of the British
firm of Jardine, Matheson and Company at Chinkiang.[21]
After Commander Joseph E. Craig replaced Goodrich, a
second uncomfortable incident occurred. Responding to
tensions brought about by Consul Fowler's efforts to save a
Japanese priest from Chinese arrest, torture, and execution,
Craig brought *Concord* into Ningpo harbor against the
wishes of local officials. "I believe that the situation demands that the flag of the United States be shown on board
a man-of-war at Ningpo," Commander Craig asserted.[22]
The anti-Western feeling resulted from American custodial
good offices and marked a case where the service led directly
to gunboat diplomacy.

Concord's escapades continued after the Ningpo affair.
The 230-foot warship returned north to Chinkiang, where
the Grand Canal crossed the Yangtze, and some junior
officers went ashore to hunt small game. Instead they acci-
dentally shot and wounded a Chinese boy, and during the
race back to the ship a pursuing Chinese band seized one of
the Americans. Only the payment of twenty Mexican dollars
to the lad's father and treatment of superficial wounds by
Concord's surgeon prevented an ugly confrontation. Consul
General Jernigan in nearby Shanghai covered up the incident. No one had been seriously hurt and no one should be
blamed for the shooting, since even the president of the
United States, that renowned sportsman, could not resist

hunting in Chinkiang were he ever to visit China. "Probably he is a better marksman," Jernigan joked uneasily, "than some of our naval officers appear to be." [23]

Despite attempts by Jernigan and Sill to gloss over the acts of bumbling Americans in China and Korea, Gresham felt gunboat diplomacy caused nothing but trouble. Several days after the *Concord* shooting, U.S. newspapers reported how the event stimulated extreme resentment and hatred for Americans in China.[24] The secretary wished to avoid any more bad publicity and criticism for the administration's Far Eastern policy. More important, these actions threatened the basis of his idealistic program of friendship and impartiality and did little to preserve peace in East Asia. He did not understand, though, that his own legalistic good offices service had contributed to the difficulties. Before Gresham could reassess gunboat diplomacy, conditions around Tientsin and Peking entangled the United States even more deeply in the Sino-Japanese War.

The Tientsin station guarding the approaches to the Chinese capital at Peking became the center of American concern during the winter of 1894–1895. Reports circulated that these two cities would be attacked by Japanese forces, and one observer declared, "Peking is panic stricken." Foreigners expected pandemonium to break loose among the unsavory elements in the city, American Board missionary William Scott Ament wrote from the capital. Concerned for the safety of their subjects, the British government evacuated women and children, and Acting Minister Denby urged Americans to follow.[25] These fears diminished, however, as the weak Manchu government prodded by foreign diplomats placed huge posters on mission walls, making it a capital crime to harass Westerners. Young Denby, anxious to divert attention from his post, claimed false dispatches had created a specter of violence. "Whatever their object, whether to justify foreign interference, or to serve other purposes," he wrote Washington, "they will cause groundless anxiety in Europe and America." [26]

The bogey of anti-Western disorder reappeared shortly

after the senior Denby returned to his ministerial post in late October 1894. Gresham trusted Denby's judgment, relied on his friend to preserve neutrality, and accepted his evaluation of the Asian situation even if it contradicted Gresham's own views. On October 31 Denby wrote the secretary and voiced his concern for the lives of sixty Americans in Peking if the Japanese marched on the capital and his belief that the United States government must provide military protection for its overseas citizens.[27]

Without waiting for Gresham's reply, Denby asked Rear Admiral Carpenter to send reinforcements to the gunboat *Monocacy* docked at Tientsin and to order its commanding officer to prepare the new men for duty in Peking. Carpenter resisted Denby's requests and cognizant of the problems his ships faced in other stations advised against supplementing *Monocacy's* crew. Not only was the 1,370-ton iron vessel, which had been built in 1863 by A. and W. Denmead and Sons of Baltimore, too unstable to accept more men on board but the force, as proposed by Denby, would be inadequate to fight its way inland to Peking. Carpenter refused to reinforce *Monocacy,* and Gresham, learning of the officer's opinion, prompted Denby to send all Americans to the nearest treaty port where the U.S. Navy could defend them. The minister insisted upon remaining in Peking and protecting the legation. Reluctantly Gresham backed up his minister and asked Secretary of the Navy Herbert to order a contingent of marines to *Monocacy*.[28]

When *Baltimore* arrived in Nagasaki on November 29, Carpenter found orders directing the assignment of additional men to the ancient gunboat. The cruiser proceeded to Chefoo where three officers and forty-two marines left the warship and boarded a British transport bound for Tientsin. The vessel arrived off the Taku Bar and waited for other merchantmen to transfer cargoes to landing lighters. The delay frustrated Captain Elliott, veteran of the march to Seoul several months before, and he landed his men unassisted by Chinese harbor officials and shuttled them to Tientsin by the local railroad. Once on Chinese territory, the marines forced their way through crowds of coolies and soldiers to the waiting train by applying "vicious blows with the butts of their pieces." Elliott later explained his action to Washington. "I was well aware I had no right to land an armed force without permission in a foreign country," he recalled, "but it was impossible for me to get this permit within necessary time, so I embarked the men and baggage on a tug." [29]

The marine guard joined *Monocacy*'s crew and awaited marching orders for Peking. Meanwhile Carpenter discussed tactics with Robert E. Impey, commander of the gunboat. Ignoring an imperial edict which forbade passage and entry of foreign soldiers into the capital, he reminded Impey of agreements with European naval representatives which might make it necessary to send an allied force to Peking. "Although arms and ammunition will be provided," Carpenter cautioned, "it is not expected that any occasion will arise for their use, and recourse to arms shall take place in an extreme emergency only such as self-defense, or the defense of the Legation against attack by an irresponsible mob." [30]

During this interval, Peking remained calm even when the Chinese stronghold at Port Arthur capitulated to Japanese invaders in November. An imperial rescript and patrols by Manchu bannermen at Christian chapels curbed anti-missionary outbreaks. "The people are so overawed by these multiplied indications of care for us on the part of the authorities," missionary spokesman William Scott Ament wrote from the capital, "that they hardly lift their eyes to a foreigner as he goes along the street for fear they will be immediately decapitated." [31] Denby exhorted Americans to stay in the city and apparently *Monocacy*'s reinforcements would not be needed after all. Then the minister learned that the Russian government had outfitted a legation guard for duty in Peking, and he prepared his own arrangements for defense of American interests. "If the other nations bring their marines hither and we bring none," he wired Gresham, "and anarchy supervenes, and mob violence breaks out, and my own people who are more numerous than any, perhaps all others, are left without protection, I should feel that I have not done my full duty." [32]

Officials in Washington read Denby's arguments but remained unconvinced. They knew the Chinese government opposed foreign intervention, and Yang warned Gresham that the introduction of additional troops into the capital would aggravate the situation. [33] Even President Cleveland, displaying a rare interest in the Sino-Japanese War, advised restraint. He regarded marines in China as a violation of his administration's nonaggressive policies of neutrality and amity toward both China and Japan. The president "thinks Carpenter's opposition to sending marines reasonable," Gresham cabled Denby, "and expects that in no event will you insist upon marines, unless other legations do." [34] Cleveland and Gresham wished to preserve American equality with other powers in China, yet hoped to maintain the image of a strict and moralistic neutral intent only on saving lives. Despite Washington's reservations, Denby arranged for American troops to march to Peking along with those of European powers. [35]

Tensions increased in February 1895, and Consul Read in Tientsin called for one hundred more men to assist *Monocacy*'s already swollen complement. Captain Elliott visited Peking and examined the abandoned Dutch legation which with its thick walls and comfortable quarters made an ideal fortified compound for his marines. At the same instant Denby informed Washington that he needed fifty marines, "in pursuance of the cooperation policy which prevails in the East." [36] Gresham realized his friend's determination to demand American armed intervention, and he forwarded a last anxious warning to the Peking legation. "I do not find in any of the treaties with China provisions authorizing the protection of the legations by foreign troops," he wrote Denby, "but if other powers bring up marines you are authorized to do the same." [37] The secretary considered such a policy dangerous, unduly aggressive, and above all else, illegal. Nevertheless he trusted Denby's good sense, integrity, and regard for duty and could offer no alternative to offset the minister's decision.

Fortunately, after months of false expectations, mob disorder failed to materialize. Charles Denby withdrew his request for marines, and in early May 1895 these reinforcements returned safely to the flagship *Baltimore*. Circumstances allowed the United States to avoid a predicament which compromised neutrality and placed American, Japanese, and Chinese lives in greater danger. The Cleveland government had been sensitive to the perils, whether real or imagined, faced by missionaries in East Asia. Moreover, good offices required additional military support if the United States expected to act as the custodian of Sino-Japanese interests. Troops had landed in Korea, a sizable fleet had engaged in protective duties, and marines had assembled for a march to Peking over the opposition of the Chinese government. Poor communications, Gresham's inexperience, and ignorance of actual conditions forced the administration to rely on policies suggested by Sill, Denby, and other diplomatic representatives in East Asia. Though the Cleveland regime had expressed reservations, it had agreed to send soldiers to Peking. It had chosen the same course which the expansionist McKinley presidency would select six years later during the Boxer Rebellion. The present administration arrived at this verdict through far different assumptions, however, than those that would govern McKinley, Roosevelt, and Secretary John Hay. In 1894 the United States had yet to occupy the Philippine Islands or take an active part in world affairs and no official open door doctrine guided diplomatic decisions. Cleveland and Gresham hoped to avoid involvement in the Sino-Japanese fight which endangered no American policy, but by pursuing an idealistic program of good offices, protection of lives and property, and the advancement of peace and order, they had come to a point where either the United States defended its policies in East Asia with force or surrendered its self-appointed position as custodian of Chinese and Japanese interests. Withdrawal now, after building up the navy in Asian waters and assuming responsibilities for Oriental lives, would destroy America's moral influence and bring down the wrath of a vengeful opposition party and a critical public. Furthermore, the government must continue its good offices to mediate the conflict and perhaps bring the warring parties to the peace table.

What Will Happen to Li Hung Chang If He Loses Many More Battles. *New York World*. Reprinted from *Literary Digest*, October 1894.

5

Peacemaker

Throughout the fall and winter of 1894, the Cleveland administration confronted growing pressure to mediate the Sino-Japanese War. European nations, particularly Great Britain, urged the United States to intervene in a joint diplomatic venture to restore peace in East Asia. Lord Pauncefote frequented the State Department, reportedly bringing suggestions for an Anglo-American mediation plan. Peace groups and religious workers also asked for intercession in the terrible war. The American Peace Society even alluded to U.S. participation in an international police force which would guarantee the independence of Korea and prevent any more strife on the peninsula.[1] Dr. Henry Blodgett, a senior missionary at the North China Mission of the American Board, pleaded with Washington to end the fighting. "The American government stands in a particularly favorable position to act as peacemaker in the present dispute," Dr. Blodgett insisted, "owing to its policy of seeking no further territorial additions." [2]

The American press advanced mediation. Not only newspapers friendly to the administration but even the hostile *New York Tribune* advocated this policy. The United States as the only disinterested nation in the Far East, the *Tribune* argued, would be the ideal mediator. Other nations, especially England and Russia, coveted commercial monopoly and territory in the East, while the United States desired neither.[3] The pro-Cleveland American *Review of Reviews* agreed with the New York paper and launched its own campaign for mediation. "It has seemed to the *Review of Reviews* from the very inception of this Oriental contest that it was manifestly the duty of the United States, as a long-time friend and disinterested neighbor, to attempt to restore harmony." [4]

The Gresham-Cleveland leadership, already under attack for its earlier good-intentioned efforts to preserve peace and stability in the Far East, resisted suggestions to become further entangled. But rumors of American participation in some sort of multilateral intervention to end the war persisted. When asked by an interviewer if the United States would intervene, Assistant Secretary of State Uhl said the State Department had not received an official request for cooperation in a program of joint intervention and he refused to comment further on the subject.[5] Shortly after public denials, Uhl received a formal note from W. E. Goshen of the British legation, inquiring whether the United States would participate in a projected Western statement calling for the cessation of fighting. Uhl forwarded the communication to President Cleveland, then vacationing at Buzzards Bay, Massachusetts.

For almost a week the State Department waited for the president's answer. Worn out by the fight for tariff reduction, civil service reform, and other domestic crises, the haggard chief executive had isolated himself at his Gray Gables cottage for some fishing and much needed rest. In the summer of 1894 Cleveland suffered from ill health and was still recovering from an earlier operation for removal of a growth in his mouth. He longed to escape the decisions of public office. "It was a time when the President was under very great strain," journalist Richard Watson Gilder observed after visiting the presidential retreat.[6] He certainly could not be too concerned by what he considered a minor diplomatic issue.

Gresham, though, grew impatient and cabled his chief on October 12, "Shall I say in reply to Goshen's note copy of which was sent you that while the President earnestly desires that China and Japan shall speedily agree upon terms of peace alike honorable to both nations and not humiliating to Korea he cannot join England, Germany, Russia, and France in an intervention as requested?" [7]

Leaving the policy statement completely up to his secretary of state, Cleveland responded, "That is exactly what I was going to suggest in reply to Mr. Goshen. It is exactly right." [8] The president then returned to the nearby bay for some more fishing, and further pleadings from Goshen, assuring that any intervention would be limited to peaceful representations, were ignored.

Pressure for American mediation came next from China. On October 23 young Denby wired that the Tsungli-yamen would concede Korean independence and pay a war indemnity to Japan. The Chinese Foreign Office called for the employment of American good offices under Article I of the 1858 Treaty of Tientsin which provided for this service to bring about an amicable arrangement of a dispute between China and another nation acting oppressively or unjustly toward China. Colonel Denby arrived in Peking several days after his son's cable had been sent from China and immediately warned Gresham that the Chinese proposal contained in the message violated American neutrality. If the United States accepted Chinese mediation under Article I, Denby continued, then it would in effect recognize Japan as the aggressor and China as the innocent victim. Moreover, China had requested similar mediation from other powers and acceptance would entangle the United States in an alliance to protect the Asian country.[9]

Meanwhile in Washington, Chinese minister Yang Ju had convinced Gresham to extend good offices for mediation to China, and the secretary had cabled Denby instructing him to make such an offer. China's request and Gresham's instructions, each formulated without the knowledge of the other, arrived at their respective destinations coincidentally. Hence, China assumed that the American government had accepted the role of mediator under the terms of the Treaty of Tientsin.[10] Gresham struggled to explain this situation. Denby's wire, forwarding China's request and warning against its acceptance, he assured the minister, had arrived after the mediation offer. This exchange promised to embarrass the administration's freedom of action, and the president could not cooperate with European powers on this issue. He would serve as a peacemaker only if China and Japan selected the United States as their sole mediatory agent. If these conditions were met, Gresham wrote, then the president "will gladly aid them by conference at this capital, or in any other practicable way." [11] Cleveland hinted, however, that he might cooperate with other powers simply to determine the amount of a postwar indemnity.[12]

Gresham explained the correspondence with the Chinese to Japan and assured her that the U.S. government would not act as a mediator for China without Japan's full consent. The United States was not trying to aid China behind Japan's back, Gresham insisted, and American diplomacy would not be used to hinder Japanese war aims. "It was not until China through her minister here had repeatedly requested it," the secretary revealed, "that the President expressed his willingness to act as peacemaker." [13] He warned Japan, though, that continued warfare might force European meddling. Moved as Gresham said by "sentiments of friendship toward Japan" and not by the desire to stop Japanese military progress, he urged Japan to begin peace talks which would prevent outside interference. Minister Kurino in Washington recognized the American's partial, almost pro-Japanese tone. "I have repeated your frank statement that the United States have no policy in Asia which is endangered by the war," Kurino wrote, "and that they are actuated by sentiments of friendship toward Japan, and not in any way by a desire to retard the advance of her arms." [14] Gresham did nothing to discourage this interpretation.

The U.S. government awaited Japan's response to its proposals to mediate the conflict, and on November 13 Minister Dun reported that the imperial cabinet would take up the question. After the meeting, Japanese officials politely refused American mediatorial services, noting that while Japan appreciated the kind offer it could not achieve just and reasonable war results unless China approached Japan directly on the subject of peace negotiations. They indicated that the government would receive Chinese peace inquiries transmitted through the American legation in Peking. Thus,

while rejecting official mediation, Japan opened the door
for informal peacemaking. Though visibly tired and
strained, Gresham elected to drive out with Secretary of
the Treasury Carlisle to Cleveland's suburban Georgetown
retreat at Woodley and present Japan's reply to the president.[15]

Public discussion of Japan's repudiation of American
mediation coincided with earlier attitudes toward the service, and those who had favored it accepted the rebuff
philosophically. They found nothing offensive to the United
States in Japan's refusal to take advantage of the good
offices of a benevolent peacemaker. After all, American
diplomats could still function as messengers, if not formal
mediators, and even this limited duty would project the
United States into the center of the peace negotiations.
Consequently it could benefit from its treaty role without
assuming the thankless office of legal intermediary. "The
spectacle of the United States as the friend of all peoples,
referred to without question as an unprejudiced mediator
in the quarrels of nations, is one of which Americans should
be proud. We not only keep the peace ourselves, but we are
trusted peacemakers in all parts of the world." [16] Opponents
of mediation and antiadministration critics, on the other
hand, cited Japanese rejection as evidence of more diplomatic bungling and a natural result of Gresham's inept
Far Eastern policies. The war was none of America's business and the secretary's communications constituted an
officious piece of meddling which interfered with Japan's
civilizing crusade in China.[17]

Futile debate over the failure of mediation ignored
efforts to bring the Asian combatants to the peace table now
being performed by U.S. diplomats in the war zone. China
and Japan had accepted good offices early in the war and
Americans had performed a number of unofficial services
for both belligerents. Acting as a messenger to keep lines
of communication open between hostile parties was one of
the legal functions of the original offer, and in late 1894
the East Asian governments began transmitting messages
to each other through American diplomatic representatives.

For several critical months between November 1894 and
the final peace arrangements in April 1895, Ministers
Denby and Dun, Consul Read, and Consul William H.
Abercrombie in Nagasaki served as the only means of diplomatic contact approved by both warring parties. No other
nation shared this responsibility.

Secretary Gresham considered this messengerial assistance a proper adjunct of the administration's good offices
policy during the Sino-Japanese War. It permitted belligerent statesmen to discuss their differences, transmit dispatches, and helped bring about peace talks which might
forestall European intervention. Gresham believed the
government had moral obligations to perform this duty as
long as it did not lead to complications which might compromise neutrality and amicable relations with both nations.
A correct application of good offices required complete
impartiality and the silent transfer of diplomatic notes.
American officials could not offer advice or comment on
the contents of dispatches. It was illegal for any U.S.
diplomat to serve a foreign government while still holding
office, and Gresham determined not to permit this dangerous double standard.

Unfortunately Minister Denby did not share Gresham's
narrow, legalistic interpretation of messengerial good offices.
From the outset, he saw his position as an opportunity to
change the course of East Asian history and to increase
American influence in the area. China stood on the brink
of a profound and historic transformation, Denby told
Gresham, and the United States must participate in the
shaping of a new China. Without waiting for the secretary's
reply, Denby prepared to follow his own advice and in
November 1894 asked the Tsungli-yamen to give him the
power to present China's peace proposals directly to Japan.[18]

The Chinese Foreign Office wished to employ the anxious
American for its own purposes, but first it watched as Li
Hung-chang tried to deal directly with Japan by dispatching
his private emissary, customs commissioner Gustav Detring,
on a mission of peace to the islands. Li's German-born provincial adviser carried a letter to Japanese Prime Minister

Viscount Ito Hirobumi. Japan ignored Detring, refused Li's message, and stated that the German had not received proper credentials from the Chinese government to discuss peace and would not be recognized in any capacity. As Minister Kurino in Washington claimed, Japan had rebuffed Detring not from any desire to prolong war but because it hoped to ensure the success of any peace negotiations by forcing China to send a fully accredited envoy.[19]

Colonel Denby assumed the credit for Detring's failure. "When I undertook to negotiate on the part of China to bring about peace the Chinese Government immediately recalled Mr. Detring." [20] Denby's part in peace preliminaries became important enough without his exaggerations since Japan's treatment of Li's private emissary implied that it would talk with China only through the American legation in Peking and this left Denby in the key position to transmit and receive all peace proposals. The Chinese Foreign Office turned to the American to interpret Japanese diplomatic maneuvering and to assist the Yamen in the formulation of appropriate responses. Although he never became an official mediator, Denby did serve as an intimate adviser for the Chinese on technical and substantive matters during peace preliminaries with Japan. In fact, he found it difficult to convince the Tsungli-yamen that he could not conduct all negotiations for China. "They even asserted that their Minister at Washington had wired that the President had consented that I should act for them as commissioner to make peace," Denby revealed to Gresham in December 1894.[21]

Despite assertions to the contrary, Denby performed all the diplomatic functions of a mediatory agent short of actually going to Japan and sitting down at the peace table. When Dun cabled Japan's terms for opening conversations to end the war, Denby told the Yamen that it had only two options in response to Japan's cable—China could either decline the terms outright or it could appoint a fully accredited ambassador extraordinary and minister plenipotentiary for the purpose of negotiation. China procrastinated, requesting Denby to cable Japan for further information. The Yamen instructed him to inform the Japanese government that China would not designate a representative until Japan indicated exactly what the two countries were going to discuss. He forwarded this desultory response but, after Dun sent Japan's impatient reply, warned China to accept Japanese terms and comply with their demands. "I pointed out that the war would now go on at the expense of China," Denby cabled the State Department, "and while I wished to leave the Yamen perfectly free to carry on war or make peace still it was my duty, as they consulted me as an adviser, to say that unless they hoped to gain great successes in the future it would be better to make peace." [22]

China agreed to appoint a minister with full powers to negotiate peace and offered to hold talks in Shanghai. Tokyo refused to meet on Chinese soil and stated it would name its own plenipotentiary only after China's peace ambassador had set foot in Japan and presented his credentials. These arrangements humiliated China since in its long history it had never negotiated a treaty on foreign territory, and the Yamen turned again to Denby for suggestions hoping at the same time to share some of the burden for surrender with the American. The U.S. minister recommended compliance with every Japanese order and explained patiently that international law required a defeated nation to accept the site of negotiations from the victor. Moreover, in a promise which later haunted him, he assured the Yamen that Chinese officials would not be harmed if they journeyed to Japan.[23]

Denby thought the Foreign Office had succumbed to the inevitable when it appointed two peace commissioners on December 20. But China also could play the subtle Oriental game of saving face and selected two minor bureaucrats, one of them noted for his payment of reward money for the taking of Japanese heads, expressly for the purpose of affronting Japan. Nevertheless, as Dun noted, Japan feared European intervention in the war, desired peace, and would meet the Chinese plenipotentiaries.[24] China's decision to at last sit down around a peace table pleased Denby. He had done all he could to bring the two nations together, he assured Gresham, and without his guidance China might never look for peace. "I have, alone, done the troublesome and difficult work of inducing China to sue for peace," Denby boasted; "jealousy, distrust, ill feeling in and out of the Yemen had to be overcome." [25]

The minister's function as an adviser and intermediary continued, and he forwarded China's request for the names of Japan's plenipotentiaries and inquired as to the exact spot for the mission to land in Japan. Growing tired of China's constant delay, Japan replied bluntly to Denby's notes. This supposed rudeness angered the American, and he demanded that Dun inform the Japanese government about his unnecessary humiliation. Dun relayed the message to Foreign Minister Mutsu who brushed Denby's complaints aside. Acting more like an insulted Chinese bureaucrat than an impartial American messenger, Colonel Denby rushed a note directly to the Japanese statesman, ordering Japan to treat China more gently.[26] Mutsu politely ignored Denby. The incensed U.S. minister, insisting that neither Japan nor China pursued peace along accepted lines of Western diplomacy, asked Washington to intervene and direct the negotiations. "It would be advisable for the Department to consider whether supervision should be had of the treaty-making process," Denby cabled, "and whether good result might follow friendly suggestions made in the interest of the treaty powers." [27]

All along Denby had assured Gresham of the limited nature of his messengerial function, and the secretary had left him alone. Gresham had known the colonel for over two decades, in fact ever since the men had been lawyers together back in Indiana, and he trusted the minister. He expected him to follow administration policies and believed Denby carried out a strictly impartial and correct diplomacy. But Gresham had doubted the wisdom of Denby's position during the Peking marine question, and though he supported the minister, this latest unwanted advice and direct appeal to Japan tried Gresham's patience. At last Denby had gone too far and endangered Japanese-American friendship and threatened the administration's neutral position. The secretary ordered Denby to do nothing to compromise this policy.[28] Under pressure from his chief, the minister attempted to make amends and explained how his contributions to China had been simply an unofficial act of kindness. He had not upset administration neutrality, but if the secretary was dissatisfied with his actions, he would "severely heed the admonition." [29]

While Gresham tried to curb his exuberant minister in China, back in Washington he received a surprise visit from another old family acquaintance, former Secretary of State John Watson Foster. Though Foster had served Gresham's hated foe Benjamin Harrison and differed with the current government's antiexpansionist program, the secretary still considered Foster a friend and welcomed him to the department. The warm greeting faded though as Foster announced his intention of assisting China in its peace negotiations with Japan. "He told me he established friendly relations with one of the Chinese envoys while he was Minister here," Gresham wrote Ambassador Bayard, "and that through that influence, he, Foster, was employed to assist in conducting the negotiations for peace." [30]

Foster informed Gresham that he would leave for East Asia next Friday and would like one of the department clerks to accompany him. The secretary absolutely refused to help a private citizen interfere in the diplomacy of the Sino-Japanese War. He was disappointed that Foster, a respected international legal expert, could not see that his intervention threatened American neutrality just as much as any illegal act by less honorable men. Moreover, Gresham believed Foster's interest in the negotiations was purely financial. The ex-secretary had visited China the previous year, had toured the Kaiping mines and railroads, and had observed the rich investment opportunities in the region. The former diplomatic leader had dabbled already in several questionable profit-making schemes in the Far East, including the illegal infernal-machine plot several months before. His name had been linked to those of Delaware entrepreneur James Harrison Wilson and Li's private secretary and intimate adviser William N. Pethick in an alleged plan to overthrow the Manchu dynasty and make Li Hung-chang the ruler of China.[31] Unaware of all the details, Gresham had received some information concerning Foster's machinations along with those of a former State Department employee in China named Chester Holcombe to raise a $400,000,000 loan in silver for China. "You can readily see that if Foster is not already a very rich man," Gresham told Bayard, "his prospects for becoming a millionaire are flattering." [32]

Though Gresham had divorced the government from Foster's most recent scheme, administration critics still used the Foster-Gresham meeting to further embarrass the secretary. Senator William M. Stewart of Nevada, an ardent expansionist, called upon the Senate to investigate Gresham's apparent complicity with the former secretary of state and introduced a resolution requiring him to inform the Senate whether Foster had any official relations in assisting China in the peace negotiations with Japan.[33] Senator Morgan of Alabama defended the administration. "I think it well enough to pass the resolution," Morgan argued, "though I can state on the authority of General Foster that his mission to China, or Japan rather, has no connection in the world with any official act, or recognizance even, of the United States Government." [34] Gresham similarly assured the Senate, but his explanation hardly served to curb attacks on his foreign policy.

In his handling of the Foster affair and in his instructions to Denby, Gresham determined not to open new avenues of antiadministration criticism and provide a platform for opponents of his Far Eastern diplomacy. He had failed in this endeavor and his resentment of Foster and Denby grew. Both men embarrassed the government, and the U.S. messengerial service promised to lead to the same crisis posed months earlier by the protection of belligerent property and lives. What had started out as a moral, correct, and humane policy had prompted illegal acts by two respected individuals, both former trusted compatriots of the secretary.

Confused, tired, and in poor health, Gresham wished for
an end to this perplexing East Asian war which corrupted
the morals of honest men.

Fortunately, toward the end of January 1895 Denby
reported progress in Sino-Japanese peace negotiations, and
the termination of fighting seemed close. Japan and China,
Gresham hoped, would have no further need for American
good offices. Contrary to his expectations though, as a
cease-fire drew near Denby actually increased his participation in the preliminary negotiations. He drafted a set
of credentials for the Chinese peace envoys which included
the words "plenipotentiaries with full powers" and which
he expected Japan to accept as the basis for the beginning
of substantive peace talks. The Chinese negotiators, supposedly invested with proper diplomatic authority, left
Shanghai on January 26 and arrived in Kobe on the
thirtieth. John W. Foster, already in Japan, met the envoys
at the dock and examined their instructions. As he later
recorded in his memoirs, the letters were "not in the usual
form among nations" and he imagined the Japanese would
refuse them.[35] Prime Minister Ito and Foreign Minister
Mutsu, Japan's peace team, did indeed renounce the directive as defective and unsatisfactory and unleashed a propaganda tirade against Chinese duplicity.[36]

The Chinese party, accompanied by Foster, returned to
China, and as one American editor suggested, "even the
ornate whiskers of our own John W. Foster couldn't per-
suade the Japanese authorities to accept the credentials of
those envoys from China." [37] Denby took this latest diplomatic failure as a personal misfortune. China's dispatches
were his dispatches and he could no longer separate the two.
The legitimate messenger had become a servant and pawn
of the Tsungli-yamen. Denby defended himself and argued
that Japan had rejected his credentials because the Chinese
had substituted their own ambiguous version for his and
had removed any reference to full powers for signing a
peace treaty. The American castigated the Yamen for its
apparent deception, since he refused to become the scape-
goat for its surrender to Japanese terms. The Chinese must

let him correct any future dispatches, Denby insisted. "I demanded that any new letters of credence prepared by the Yamen should be submitted to me before transmission," Denby told his government, "and they agreed to this demand." [38]

At last China surrendered to Japanese pressure and Denby's exhortations by appointing aging statesman Li Hung-chang, governor of Chihli Province and commander of Chinese forces in the war with Japan, as the sole plenipotentiary with full powers to treat for peace. After the initial Japanese victories in the conflict, the throne had removed Li's yellow jacket and peacock feather, signs of imperial favor, but now restored them to him before his journey for peace to Japan. The Yamen viewed Li's appointment with pleasure since he would be held responsible for China's humiliation and not the Foreign Office. The gullible American minister might also be employed to divert attention from the weaknesses of China's foreign policies, and the Yamen begged him to urge the president of the United States to ask Japan for an end to all fighting.[39] But this time Denby refused to be lured into further entanglements, particularly since he now learned from Minister Dun in Tokyo that Japan refused to discuss the credentials question any longer. The Japanese would not accept Li's mission, Dun warned Denby, unless he had full powers to recognize the complete independence of Korea, the cession of territory, the opening of trade, and any additional demands Japan might present later. The Japanese government instructed Dun to ascertain whether China understood these conditions and would comply with them before dispatching any new emissary.[40]

Li Hung-chang delayed answering Japan, hoping in the meantime to draw some Western power into the negotiations. The United States still appeared a likely candidate, though he also contacted British, Russian, German, and French diplomats. Li visited Denby on February 21 and solicited American help in persuading Japan to discuss a cease-fire. He asked the minister to use his influence with Japan to befriend China. Denby replied "flatly and firmly," he assured Washington, "that my Government would in no wise intervene in the war, nor interfere in any way between the two nations." [41] Li evidently received more favorable responses from certain European representatives in Peking and established the groundwork for the later tripartite intervention. If Li had wrung commitments from other powers, he did not tell the American minister since Denby cabled Washington that Li had not obtained any support.[42] He suspected intrigues, though, and went to see the elder statesman and warned him that European intervention would lead to China's dismemberment and that she must look for future cooperation from the United States to resist this aggression. He envisaged the two nations, joined perhaps by Japan, working together to build a progressive, modern, and enlightened postwar East Asia without European interference. This great end could be accomplished, Denby concluded, only if China now surrendered to Japan.[43]

After his meeting with Western representatives, Li Hungchang prepared his peace entourage for the trip to Japan. Accompanied by over 150 attendants and officials, traveling in two steamships, Li expected to impress the Japanese with the size and splendor of his retinue. An American missionary in Japan commented, "If he had taken his grip in hand and set out alone in a canoe, he would have made quite as strong an impression, as the Japanese are not likely to be overawed by anything a Chinaman can now get up in the way of display, and he would have more money left toward paying the indemnity that Japan will exact." [44] In any case on March 20, 1895, Li and his procession arrived at Shimonoseki, a heavily garrisoned port city just across the straits from the Korean peninsula and the site selected by Japan for the conference which would begin the following day.

Several days later Li discussed peace terms with Viscount Ito and Minister Mutsu and requested an armistice. The Japanese demanded, instead, the Chinese surrender of the remaining fortifications and arsenals around Peking. If China accepted these terms, as well as paying the expenses of the peace conference, then Japan would consider an armistice. When news of these conditions reached the Yamen, it asked Denby's impressions and the American minister offered some unofficial advice which urged China's complete surrender. "I said this was severe but if they thought China could not defend these places they should accept." [45] This time the Chinese ignored Denby's counsel and resisted Japan's ultimatum by ordering Li to refuse the armistice terms. These proposals, the Yamen complained, would render Peking utterly defenseless. [46]

Li met with the Japanese envoys and rejected their conditions for a cease-fire. The ancient Chinese leader then entered his open sedan chair for the trip back to his apartment when suddenly a young Japanese fanatic rushed from the crowd and fired a small-caliber pistol point-blank at the diplomat's face. The tiny slug entered just below Li's left eye, lodged in his cheekbone, and foreign surgeons expressed grave concern for the elder gentleman's life. Observers, expecting the worst, awaited further news. The president "has heard with profound regret of this most deplorable occurrence," Gresham informed Yang, "and earnestly hopes that the distinguished sufferer may speedily recover from the effects of his wound." [47]

Li's foreign legal adviser John W. Foster arrived at the wounded envoy's quarters as the surgeons probed for the embedded bullet. The old man grasped the American's hand and asked him to return later. That evening the remarkably alert and much recovered Chinese leader held a private conversation with Foster and their interpreters. Denby had deceived him, Li charged, by assuring him there would not be the slightest danger of assassination or violence in Japan. He no longer trusted Denby and now relied more heavily on his foreign friends Foster, Detring, and William N. Pethick, a former vice-consul and interpreter at the American consulate in Tientsin and Li's personal tutor and close adviser. Foster remained at Li's side, calming his anger at Japan for the heinous attempt on his life. The attack, he promised Li, "would turn out for the benefit of China, as Japan would be less exacting in its terms." [48]

The assassination attempt ended official American good offices in China for the time being, although U.S. diplomats later helped in the ratification of the peace treaty. This in turn freed the United States from participation in the compromises Japan would permit as a result of the shooting. After months of informal mediation by U.S. diplomats and direct negotiation by private Americans, Japan and China agreed finally to discuss peace arrangements. Denby, Dun, Foster, and others did not influence the ultimate outcome, but they played a major part in bringing the belligerents together. Their peacemaking enthusiasm, though, threatened Gresham's policies and strained further the limits of good offices and strict neutrality.[49]

Japan (to China): "Come on, John; let's show them that we're just as advanced Christians as they are." *Chicago Journal.* Reprinted from *Literary Digest,* August 1894.

6

The Pigtail War

Gresham and Cleveland upheld a neutral diplomacy in East
Asia during the Korean rebellion, early months of war, and
the drawn-out peace negotiations against a variety of
stresses and strains. Good offices, neutrality violations,
efforts to save Asian and American lives, and peacemaking
constantly threatened amicable and impartial relations
with the belligerents. Secretary Gresham's and to a lesser
extent President Cleveland's idealistic conduct of American
policy during the war forced the government to strengthen
the navy in the Far East, land soldiers in Korea, and come
perilously close to armed intervention in China. But perhaps
the greatest pressure on the administration's neutrality came
from public attitudes and discussion of the war in the
United States. Americans expressed a decided preference
for one side and urged the government to abandon its policy
of impartiality and back the more admirable and praise-
worthy of the two Asian combatants.

The popular caricature of Japan and China in 1894
evolved from a combination of press releases, editorials,
journal articles, and Oriental propaganda. Treatments of
the war ranged over such topics as the belligerents' racial
characteristics, historical evolution, and military capabili-
ties. Lead articles complete with detailed maps of the war
zone and profuse illustrations of belligerent warships, land
forces, and war leaders promoted early interest in the Sino-
Japanese confrontation. Prints of China's reputed commander-in-chief Li Hung-chang, strangely resembling an
emaciated Grover Cleveland with a pigtail, as well as pic-
tures of Japanese generals, replete with medals, epaulettes,

and European-styled uniforms appeared on the pages of American dailies in every section of the country, while cartoons which included apelike representations of Chinese and Japanese soldiers tugging at each other's long, braided pigtails reflected a standard view of the adversaries. In fact the queue, a sign of Chinese subservience to the Manchu, symbolized the American attitude toward the Sino-Japanese War of 1894–1895 which most newspapers referred to contemptuously as the Pigtail War.

By the last week of July 1894 articles and editorials investigated the origins of the tension between China and Japan. According to initial commentary in U.S. newspapers, trouble started when despotic China resisted Japan's introduction of Western learning into Korea. China opposed modernization and progress while Japan supposedly offered new hope for the backward peoples of Asia. "The time has come for Japan to show herself worthy of her civilization and her ambitions," one editor wrote. "She is in Korea today for the benefit of the whole world, and her retirement therefrom would be tantamount to allowing the Hermit Kingdom to sink back to Chinese barbarism." [1] China dominated Korea so completely, editor William Randolph Hearst claimed, that today the pitiful kingdom "is as near to an absolute nonentity as any aggregation of ten million people could possibly become without flickering out of existence. It is a colorless and feeble copy of China." [2]

Assuming that Japan represented progress and a better world, most writers supported the island empire from the beginning. In a theme which recurred throughout the war, Americans equated Japan's national experience with that of their own country and the Japanese people with their U.S. counterparts. Ignoring earlier Japanese contacts with the Dutch and other Europeans, they believed the United States had introduced Japan to the Western world when Commodore Matthew C. Perry had visited the islands in 1853. Again disregarding German, British, and French influences on Japan's late nineteenth-century modernization, American commentators claimed Japan had adopted and copied their institutions and ideas. After all, one could wander about a big Japanese city and readily recognize the American influence in the telegraph lines, efficient railroads, and modern public buildings. Smoke from huge factories and mills darkened the skies, reminding American visitors of any industrial section of their own country. Though the Asian nation looked to an emperor for leadership, it had a constitution and representative form of government believed to be just like that in the United States. Even Japanese dress appeared strikingly familiar, as businessmen attired in Western suits and top hats hurried about the bustling cities. These factors alone endeared Japan to the public, prompting one journalist to conclude, "American sympathies are doubtless with the island; the Japanese are a bright, progressive people—the Americans, so called, of Asia." [3]

Further evidence of this initial impression appeared in cultural comparisons of the combatants. Writings on race consciousness and Social Darwinism, so popular in late nineteenth-century thought, provided the framework for the discussion. Originally scholars lumped both Chinese and Japanese into something called the Mongol race and regarded both as inferior to Anglo-Saxons, allegedly because they had not evolved as completely to higher civilization. The Japanese represented the best elements of these Mongols and closely rivaled the "best of the Caucasians" but still could not be classified along with the superior forms of human development.[4] Lafcadio Hearn, expatriate American author and teacher, advanced this racial theory. Hearn, a gaunt, short man with one bad eye, had adopted Japanese dress and customs and had married a Japanese. He had rejected his native country which had not accepted his literary contributions. Japan offered a new start and fresh source of inspiration for his novels and cultural histories, and his essays on Japan sold well in the United States, helping to publicize his evolutionary thesis. Hearn termed his theory of intellectual and physical mutation, where Japanese transformed into Anglo-Saxons, "Occidentalization." It would not be long, he claimed, before they reached this supreme level of evolution.[5]

Through constant reapplication of the fanciful Occidentalization theme, Japanese appeared to grow taller and paler. The United States naturalized "hundreds of low and worthless" Europeans who were not as "white" as the Japanese, feminist Helen H. Gardener noted. This leading woman sociologist claimed that by assimilating Western technology, education, representative government, and methods of thinking, somehow Japanese had transformed their physical appearance. Now instead of studying mysterious Oriental philosophies, they devoted energy to learning American history and the English language. Throughout the Sino-Japanese War no one challenged this incredible interpretation, and most accepted the view that Japan should be "ranked with America and the nations of Western Europe, rather than with Asiatic countries." [6]

The intellectual transmutation of Japanese into Westerners made possible widespread sympathy for Japan during the war. The Asian nation had passed the tests of Western civilization which entitled it to assume an equal place beside other advanced countries. Any vestiges of foreign domination such as the unequal treaties signed in Japan's pre-civilized stage must be eradicated. The United States, accordingly, faced a moral obligation to recognize Japan's equality and defend it. Benjamin O. Flower, reformist editor of *Arena* magazine, compared Japan's struggle for recognition with the antebellum abolitionist crusade against slavery in the United States and contended that American support for Japanese progress during the war assisted enlightened and Westernized statesmen in their contest against the remnants of Oriental reaction. [7]

Observation of Japanese residing in the United States supported theories of Japan's progressiveness. When interviewed by reporters, local Japanese appeared articulate, well informed, and anxious to discuss East Asian politics with Americans. They predicted that by adopting American technology, Japan would defeat the evil forces of Chinese barbarism in the Far East. Japanese-Americans formed patriotic leagues in major U.S. cities to read war dispatches, discuss the issues, and collect contributions for their home-

land's war effort. Young students too poor to contribute
money raised brigades "armed with American rifles" and
trained in preparation for their return to fight the Chinese.
In some parts of the United States, Americans and Japanese
cooperated in a boycott of Chinese laundries and busi-
nesses.[8]

In stark contrast Chinese seemed primitive, superstitious,
corrupt, unprogressive, and the antithesis of their East
Asian neighbor. Although the Chinese people had a rich
cultural heritage, most writers accepted correspondent
Julian Ralph's impression of the Chinese as the Negroes
and Hebrews of the Orient. Drawing on a mythological
version of Afro-Americans as "Sambos," Ralph similarly
described the Chinese. "One sang an endless comic song
. . . and all laughed as long as they were awake, when they
were not wrestling or frolicking or bandying repartee with
the happy folk on passing vessels and on the shore." [9]
Press reports of Chinese in the United States huddled in
Chinatowns, praying to Joss gods, burning incense, and
singing strange "Mongolian chants" to the beat of tom-
toms reinforced Ralph's opinion. Unlike the Japanese,
Chinese residents appeared ignorant of the Asian trouble
and if they had heard reports about it they expressed a
startling indifference to the fate of their country. When
asked what the war meant to Atlanta's Chinese population,
Sam Sing, an "intelligent Atlanta Chinaman," allegedly
told a reporter, "No makee difference, Mellican Chinaman
allee samee washee, makee monee, no go war, Empler
China say come fight muchee, me no go tall, stay in Lanta,
workee, washee, no, me no go war." [10] At the same time a
Boston reporter watched the Chinese in that city's China-
town play fan-tan, only in New York, where so-called
Celestials prayed to a new god named Low Flung created
to insure victory, did any Chinese-American appear to care
what happened to China in its struggle against Japan.[11]

Early in the war Li Hung-chang remained the lone ex-
ception to the initial unfavorable impression of Chinese.
Typical views of corrupt and decadent bureaucrats did not
include Li, said to be the Bismarck of China, the greatest

of his race, and a man anxious to adopt Western education and technology. "Li Hung-chang is a man of liberal views, measured by the conservative Chinese standard," Consul Read surmised, and "is regarded as distinctly pro-foreign." [12] Li, who had emerged as one of the most powerful regional leaders in late nineteenth-century China and had placed family, friends, and colleagues in key government posts, appeared the one man capable of uniting China in a war effort against Japan since, like the great German nationalist Otto von Bismarck, he was thought to possess the ability to unite diverse groups of provinces and cities into a viable national entity. But when his many enemies urged the emperor to deprive him of his yellow jacket and peacock feather, signs of imperial favor, for permitting Japan's seizure of Seoul, Americans noted that China had repudiated a patriotic, Westernized leader.[13]

Japanese propaganda encouraged the contrasting images of Japan and China in the United States. The dissemination of pro-Japanese news began during the Korean crisis and intensified after the *Kowshing* affair. The Japanese Secret Service hired Edward Howard House, an American editor of the *Tokyo Times,* to publish material favorable to Japan. The fifty-eight-year-old House, a tall, jaundiced New Englander, had worked as a bank-note engraver, musician, and special correspondent for the *New York Tribune* and like Hearn had grown disillusioned with America, moving to Japan in 1870. For several years House taught English in a Japanese university and finally took a job with the *Times.* His anti-Western, antimissionary articles won the favor of militant Japanese leaders, and he soon became an intimate of powerful war advocates and a natural choice to push Japan's overseas propaganda campaigns.[14]

The Japanese minister in Washington and consular agents in San Francisco and New York also issued regular press releases defending their country's policies to the American public. For several months before declarations of war, Japanese had tested propaganda techniques and had tried to create favorable initial impressions of Japan to offset

Gresham's critical note to their government over Korea in July 1894. In this they succeeded, aided all the while by notions already held by Americans concerning Japan and China. As the chancellor of the Japanese consulate in New York City declared:

We are grateful to the American papers for what they say about us and for the great moral weight of the public opinion of this country, which seems to have been thrown almost entirely on the side of Japan: and whatever be the outcome of the struggle it will only strengthen the bonds between the great Republic of the Far West and her "Yankee brother," as you call Japan, of the Orient.[15]

Once war began, though, Japan made several tactical errors in its attempt to control news reaching the United States. At first it prohibited American war correspondents from accompanying its armies and angered U.S. naval personnel by tampering with and censoring the mail forwarded to the United States through Japan. But with the appointment of Kurino Shinchiro as the new Japanese minister to Washington in the latter part of August 1894, Japan effectively coordinated its propaganda program. American reporters received permission to travel with Japanese units, while Kurino improved the opinion of Japan back in the States. "I have seen a good deal of the Jap Minister, Kurino, who is a good fellow—very civilized—an ex-graduate of Harvard and a great exploiter of the press," British legation secretary Cecil Spring-Rice wrote from Washington in 1894. "He is up to all the latest American tricks." [16] The new Japanese minister countered Yang Ju's close ties with the Gresham family by cultivating friendly contacts of his own with the secretary. "Mr. Kurino told my son and myself," Mrs. Matilda Gresham recalled, "that during the Chinese-Japanese War he met Mr. Gresham almost daily, and received from him information as to what was going on in the diplomatic world." [17] Both Kurino and Yang arranged dinner parties for the Greshams, sent trinkets and mementos of friendship, and competed in attempts to convince the American leader of their country's just cause for war.[18]

Harvard-trained Kurino supervised journalistic exploitation of the war, even contributing his own timely article on the subject. Other Japanese writers supplied magazines with additional information and defended Japan's policies in Korea which had brought about war with China. They stressed Japan's social and political innovations in East Asia and told how China obstructed Japan's promotion of Western civilization. According to these publicists, Japan's policies worked toward a lasting peace in East Asia while China's intransigence meant continual unrest and warfare.[19] The same writers flattered Americans and identified Japan with ideals of justice, freedom, and liberty. As the standard-bearer of civilization and progress in the Far East, Japanese scholars told American readers, Japan pursued a mission to enlighten millions of slumbering Chinese souls. They urged American recognition and acceptance of Japan as a powerful and vital force in the world.[20]

After early discussions of the people, supplemented by continuous propaganda releases by Japan, coverage of the war turned to a comparison of the military strength of each country. On paper the Chinese army appeared awesome, for every province had its own large body of troops. Western observers late in July 1894 watched a mile-long column of dogtrotting Chinese infantry moving north toward Korea, while the rivers filled with soldier-laden boats. "A Chinese army in motion," one American reported, "can be likened to nothing more truly than a flight of locusts." [21] China can pour waves of troops into Korea for years without missing them, Dr. L. W. Luscher, a former surgeon in the Chinese navy told interviewers.[22] A statistician in the United States figured if the Japanese slaughtered a thousand Chinese a day it would take 1,500 years to kill them all.[23]

During the first weeks of war some editors and reporters expected China's estimated population of almost 400 million to overrun 40 million Japanese. China's brute strength, they predicted, would wear down the tiny island's resources since China enjoyed the strategic advantage of a land connection with the Korean battlefield while Japan would have to transport troops across a dangerous sea. "It will shortly develop," observers agreed, "that China can command advantageous positions and execute frightful slaughter once her multitudinous army spreads out on the land field." [24] Though not immediately apparent, the immensity of China proved one of the major weaknesses of that nation's war effort as each province, jealous of its own army, often refused to send troops to help Li Hung-chang fight what many considered his own private war against Japan.

Without a standardized system of armament Chinese soldiers searched for cartridges to fit their rifles, if indeed they had been furnished with firearms in the first place, since many warriors marching north carried bows and arrows and gaily decorated lances rather than modern weapons. U.S. Navy intelligence estimated that though China's banner armies listed hundreds of thousands of men only 12,000 carried effective guns and operative ammunition. [25] Chinese conscripts lacked adequate rations and uniforms while their officers pocketed payrolls and sold army provisions. The entire military system suffered from a traditional kickback duty called the squeeze and which journalist Julian Ralph found as corrupt as the American Tammany plan. [26] These same ill-provided soldiers clung to a variety of ancient superstitions such as eating black dog flesh and ground tiger bones to make them brave. [27]

The Japanese army by comparison seemed a model of efficiency. In 1879 General Ulysses S. Grant, stopping in East Asia on his trip around the world, had predicted that Japanese troopers were so well trained and armed that 10,000 of them could march against all odds back and forth across China. [28] This army was even better in 1894. Westerners praised Japan's conscription system and carefully organized active and reserve armies which stood at 65,000 in peacetime but could be expanded immediately to over 200,000 in the event of war. Drilling in modern uniforms, each man armed with Japanese-made, repeating Murata rifles, Japanese infantry reflected the training and discipline of their former European instructors. Officers memorized modern textbooks on tactics and longed to try the theories in battle, and the entire army equipped with the latest artillery and supported by the best supply and hospital corps in the world impatiently anticipated the test of combat.[29]

A few American observers recognized the superior Japanese war preparations. Captain William R. Bridgman, former commander of the cruiser *Baltimore* on the Asiatic Station, dispelled fears of Japanese inundation by China's mass armies. Unless China mobilized quickly, which the veteran officer doubted, Japan's splendid navy and army would defeat China. After hearing Bridgman's predictions, American editors forecast a Japanese victory, and as one journalist prophesied, Japan's fighting man promised "hot work for his pig-tailed enemies." [30]

This evaluation of Japan's military potential received its first major trial in August at P'yongyang (the contemporary press called it Ping Yang), an ancient walled stronghold dominating the road through northern Korea to Manchuria. The Chinese reinforced the massive palisades with loop-holed and moated earthworks, garrisoned by picked soldiers armed with repeating rifles, and the six Chinese and Manchu generals flying their banners at P'yongyang expected their lines of infantry, artillery, and select Manchurian cavalry to check the invading Japanese "dwarf men." When 14,000 Japanese troops attacked, Chinese forces resisted for a time, but then superbly disciplined invaders forced them to abandon the strategic city and retreat across the Yalu River leaving Japan in control of the Korean peninsula.[31]

News of the Battle of P'yongyang first reached the United States through pro-Chinese dispatches transmitted to London from Shanghai and Tientsin and then sent on to New York City. These cables announced a Chinese victory, but several days later Central News Agency reports, which refuted the initial declaration, arrived and claimed a complete triumph for Japan. Americans believed the latter version and blamed inaccurate, premature accounts of the contest on the Reuters news service, said to "foist" information cooked in London off on the U.S. press. New York newspapers began to rely on the United Press Service which provided Central News Agency dispatches from Tokyo and set the tone for most of the war news printed in other American dailies across the country, thus assuring pro-Japanese press treatment.[32] *Public Opinion* magazine surveyed leading editorials from Boston to San Francisco and reported a consensus of writers that Japan had won respect, admiration, and equality among civilized nations by her actions at P'yongyang.[33]

A few voiced concern over Japan's easy victory. American missionaries in Japan, fearing a loss of influence because of Japan's new sense of superiority, expressed misgivings as their spokesman Dwight W. Learned in Tokyo explained how the victory reinforced Japan's resolve to replace Western advisers, teachers, and preachers with its own people. The island people believed they had a mission to lead all Asia, he complained, and "after regenerating China to stimulate aid to India for independence." [34] Several journalists warned that the triumph had engendered a spirit of unhealthy militarism which posed a threat to the United States, and they deplored praise for Japan which had become nothing more than a scientific murderer.[35]

These minority opinions soon faded as news of a monumental naval battle fought off the mouth of the Yalu River reached the United States. In this most hotly contested encounter of the Sino-Japanese War, over a dozen modern, foreign-built, steel Japanese cruisers and smaller vessels exchanged fire for six hours with a similar number of Chinese warships, including two 7,430-ton German-built battleships. One, the *Chen Yüan,* which boasted four twelve-inch guns and a fourteen-inch armor belt, alone sustained 400 hits from Japanese rapid-firing cannon. Former Annapolis midshipman Philo Norton McGiffen, an adviser on the Chinese battleship, reported Japanese cruisers armed with modern batteries "riddled the Chinese superstructure with them, disabling unprotected guns, and driving their crews away, besides setting on fire boats and all woodwork in unprotected parts of the ship." Japanese shells, though, could not penetrate the armor belt, and as dusk settled around the smoke-obscured battle area the Japanese fleet withdrew.[36]

Although Japanese naval guns failed to sink *Chen Yüan* and her sister ship *Ting Yuan,* Japan's navy recorded another victory. At Yalu, Japanese cruisers and torpedo boats sank four Chinese ships, the 3,500-ton Armstrong ram cruisers *Ch'ao Yung* and *Yang Wei* and the 2,300-ton steel cruisers *Chih Yüan* and *King Yüan,* without the loss of a single warship. The remnants of the demoralized Chinese fleet limped into Port Arthur for repairs and never again emerged as an important factor in the war. Though the Chinese Peiyang squadron, which had fought at Yalu, still existed and a larger southern squadron never even entered the fight, Japan now effectively controlled the sea routes to China and northern Korea.[37]

The U.S. government learned by ciphered telegram on September 19, 1894, about this historic battle between modern steel warships. Acting Minister Denby, possessing sketchy information as usual, thought the Chinese had lost five ships and the Japanese three. Commander Robert E. Impey of *Monocacy* then at Tientsin provided more accurate information, including the names of the Chinese ships believed lost. The Japanese legation in Seoul declared that Japan had destroyed eleven enemy warships but then lowered the estimate while admitting her own warships had suffered damage. By September 21, when all these reports became public, cables transmitted from Tokyo convinced Americans that Japan had not lost a single ship at Yalu.[38]

The Navy Department in Washington recognized the importance of this large naval battle between modern iron-clads and steel warships, and Secretary Herbert ordered Rear Admiral Carpenter to gather intelligence about the sea fight. He commanded the officer to steam close to crippled Chinese men-of-war and inspect damage. "You are vested with ample power to obtain accurate information either by sending ships or special details of officers for such purpose," Herbert wired Carpenter, "and it is important that the

Department shall learn, at the earliest possible moment, all lessons taught by the naval battles that have been or may be fought during the present war." [39] The secretary promised additional warships to facilitate this mission and considered for a time dispatching assistant naval constructor Richmond P. Hobson to the war zone, but line officers who wanted one of their own to go instead discouraged Herbert. Hobson later explained the problem to his uncle. "An application last fall to be ordered to the seat of war between China and Japan, at first favorably received by the Secretary," he remembered, "aroused opposition in the service, and was finally denied." [40]

Herbert read intelligence reports carefully and collected newspaper clippings on the Yalu battle in a thick scrapbook. He studied a confidential letter about the fight forwarded to him by Theodore Roosevelt. "I don't feel at liberty to give the name of the writer," Roosevelt wrote, "but you may rely absolutely that what he says is so. He is a trained military expert whose business it is to observe and record such facts as these." [41] It was later revealed that the military expert was Speck von Sternburg, German military attaché in Peking and confidant of the future president of the United States. Herbert also examined firsthand accounts of the battle from Philo N. McGiffen, an eccentric person with staring eyes who years before had been asked to leave the United States Naval Academy at Annapolis for a combination of disciplinary and academic reasons. Like House and Hearn, men who felt discarded by their own country, McGiffen found a new life in East Asia and became a naval instructor in China. When Sino-Japanese warfare erupted he was assigned to the *Chen Yüan* as an adviser and suffered concussions and other wounds during the Yalu fight which destroyed his health and gradually his mind. McGiffen returned to the United States, head swathed in bandages and leaning heavily on a cane, claiming that he was now the world's leading authority on naval warfare. At first Americans honored him; journalist Richard Harding Davis called him a great hero, and he was invited to lecture on the battle at the Naval War College in Rhode Island. But

McGiffen made astounding assertions of his contributions and at times babbled incoherently. Eventually he would be laughed at and would retire to a veteran's hospital where he would commit suicide with his own service revolver.[42]

In 1849 Herbert respected both McGiffen's and Sternburg's observations. They commented on the invincibility of the battleships and declared that if these giant warships had been commanded by able officers and had been supplied with enough shells Chinese ships would have defeated the Japanese at Yalu. Secretary Herbert adopted their conclusions in an article on the fight which he prepared for the *North American Review,* a journal noted for its expansionist and "big navy" views. In his essay, Herbert argued that the United States Navy must have large, heavily armored warships if it hoped to become a major naval power. His pleas for the construction of an American battleship fleet did not become as famous as those of Captain Mahan, but the Japanese Imperial Navy considered the *Review* article important enough to translate and distribute to its naval officers.[43]

Herbert also employed information gathered about Yalu to promote the "New Navy" and to reorganize department bureaus. The secretary cited the lessons of Yalu in his recommendations for additional ships, improved armament, and refurbished supply facilities. The sea battle revealed the strength of battleships and the utility of torpedo boats, he contended, and proved the superiority of rapid-fire guns. He recommended the construction of two new battleships and twelve torpedo boats and told the president, "We are not in want of ordinary unarmored cruisers or gunboats, but we are lamentably deficient in torpedo boats, and we certainly need more battleships." [44] In his annual report for 1894, Herbert also mentioned Yalu as the basis for his suggestions that all combustible materials be removed from American warships, such as elaborate wooden trim.[45]

The Yalu conflict influenced Herbert's thinking about departmental reorganization. Despite Secretary Benjamin F. Tracy's and William C. Whitney's earlier reforms, the

Navy Department still contained too many bureaus with overlapping responsibilities for supplying parts, ammunition, and other necessary articles to maintain the fleet at sea. Waste, delay, and confusion permeated the naval estab- lishment, and Herbert wanted to clean up obsolete hard- ware lying around in naval yards, as well as to consolidate functions in some of the eight bureaus. The Chinese had failed to solve these problems, Herbert suggested, and had run short of vital supplies at the height of the naval engage- ment. "A nation, the most populous in the world, able to put millions of fighting men into the field," Herbert con- cluded, "is now, after suffering many disasters, scouring Europe and America for munitions of war." [46]

Other naval men shared Herbert's intense interest in Yalu. The United States Naval Institute in Annapolis published an article on the battle in its *Proceedings,* and the Naval War College and Torpedo School at Newport, Rhode Island, offered six papers on the Sino-Japanese War, including three by crippled veteran McGiffen. Surgeon General J. P. Tryon of the N.S. Navy discussed the heavy casualties aboard ship and called for the construction of an ambulance ship. "Had either of the fleets in the naval battle off Yalu been in possession of such a vessel," Tryon noted, "the casualties by drowning caused by the sinking of the *Chen Yuen* [it was damaged but not sunk] would no doubt have been greatly decreased." [47] Rear Admiral Rich- ard W. Meade, commander of the North Atlantic Station in 1894, referred to the East Asian naval encounter in a paper delivered before a meeting of naval architects and constructors in New York and called for the building of new battleships and 100 torpedo boats.[48] Even Mahan, then captain of the cruiser *Chicago* stationed in English waters, commented on Yalu in a press interview. A nation cannot hope to fight a war, Mahan proclaimed, without a "fleet in being," and as he told his friend in the Royal Engineers, Major Sir George Clarke, the Asian battle reinforced his theories about the influence of seapower upon history.[49]

While naval specialists discussed technical aspects of Yalu, the public expressed excitement over Japan's so-called

Trafalgar and claimed Japan had won because they employed Annapolis-trained officers and strategies developed by Captain Mahan. "Looking on the tactics and results as a whole," one exuberant editor recorded, "they are flattering to Americans, for the Japanese are pupils of Captain Mahan and the Chinese are not; and our navy's strength is in cruisers, gunboats, etc., and not in ironclads." Actually Japan had sent only six officers to the U.S. Naval Academy since 1873, had employed French and British ships and tactics, and Mahan had advocated battleship fleets rather than cruisers, but this did not matter to a public who viewed Japan as an American protégé.[50]

Public interest in the Sino-Japanese War declined after the Battle of Yalu. The Japanese seemed to be marching to victory in an efficient and commendable manner. They had learned to fight war along Western lines and soon would carry the conflict to a just and honorable conclusion against their decadent foe. So far the island people had done nothing to alter this confident and friendly view. The *Kowshing* affair early in the war had been a regrettable mistake, quickly forgotten. But then James Creelman, the aggressive correspondent for Joseph Pulitzer's muckraking *New York World,* revealed an Asian atrocity story which focused American attention once more on Eastern Asia and challenged the smug complacency about Japan's supposed superior civilization.

James Creelman, handsome, immaculately dressed and groomed even in a war zone, was determined to become the world's most famous correspondent, a goal in part inspired by early frustrations experienced as a writer for James Gordon Bennett's *New York Herald.* Bennett's policies prevented Creelman's signature from appearing on his articles and, chafing under this restriction, the ambitious reporter left the *Herald* in 1890. Three years later he became manager of *Cosmopolitan Magazine*'s British edition and the following year accepted an assignment as special correspondent for the *New York World* to cover the Sino-Japanese War. Creelman went anywhere and did anything for a news scoop and at one time or other interviewed

Indian chieftains, Mexican dictators, European revolution-
aries, feuding Kentucky families, brooding Russian nov-
elists, and even the Pope. The Asian war, though, provided
one of his most difficult and dangerous assignments. At
P'yongyang he pitched his tent among rotting corpses to
cover the battle, and in order to catch Japanese units before
the attack on Port Arthur he rode a military pony all night
arriving on the verge of collapse yet thankful he had not
missed the opening shots. Several times Creelman narrowly
escaped capture and possible torture by Chinese patrols
because he insisted on rushing ahead of Japan's front lines
to study the action.[51]

Everywhere Creelman worked he stirred up controversy.
As the American minister to Seoul reported, the journalist
tended to overdramatize conditions in Korea and deliber-
ately misinterpreted information gathered in an interview
with the Korean king to provide more sensational copy.[52]
Creelman's early articles from East Asia, however, created
little controversy and simply praised the Japanese as
courageous and patriotic soldiers who should be admired
by the world.[53] Then for a mônth the journalist dropped
out of sight and rumors circulated that Creelman had been
slain. Fearing the worst, Pulitzer hired E. H. House to send
war dispatches to the *World* and to discover whether a
foreign correspondent killed at the front was Creelman.[54]

Creelman had not communicated with New York because
he journeyed aboard a Japanese troopship accompanying
the Port Arthur invasion force. Port Arthur, situated at the
extremity of the Liaotung Peninsula, presented Japan with
its most formidable enemy fortification. Designed by
German engineers, including Colonel von Hanneken of
Kowshing fame, the walls of the bastion which overlooked
dry docks, shipyards, and repair shops, extended in some
places as much as 300 feet out of the sea. The forts contained a deadly array of heavy naval rifles, particularly
forty- and fifty-ton Krupp batteries and rifled mortars. Even
the Japanese high command considered attack from the
sea impossible but knew that as long as the modern naval
base guarded the Strait of Chihli and sheltered the Peiyang

squadron, supply lines to Manchuria would never be completely secure. Therefore Port Arthur must be captured, and Japanese strategists drew up a bold plan to land an army above the city, march it around behind the forts, and besiege them from the land side.[55]

The Japanese attacked Port Arthur on November 21, and resistance with a few exceptions collapsed as assaulting infantry advanced under the cover of their mountain artillery. The Chinese defenders fled. As they approached the walls of the last palisades, Japanese soldiers discovered the mutilated heads of their captured comrades hanging by strings from the main gate of the fort. When they entered the city, the Japanese found all the combatants gone and bent upon revenge turned on the civilian population in an orgy of slaughter and torture. Creelman, who had landed with the invasion force, accompanied the army into the city and observed the brutality. The Japanese "killed everything they saw," he reported. "Unarmed men, kneeling in the streets and begging for life, were shot, bayoneted, or beheaded. . . . the town was sacked from end to end, and the inhabitants were butchered in their own homes." [56] Officers permitted the slaughter, Creelman charged, while soldiers laughed and played with the victims' severed heads. By the journalist's estimate over 2,000 helpless civilians had been cut down, and only Chinese coolies needed to bury the dead survived the massacre.[57]

News of Port Arthur's collapse reached the United States almost immediately, Colonel Denby cabling Gresham the information on November 24. Reports of the atrocities, however, remained rumor for several weeks as initial reports reflected recent American approval of Japan's modern tactics and superior civilization. London dispatches which alluded to brutality and slaughter by Japanese at Port Arthur received little notice in the New York press. No one took the British revelations seriously since Americans believed that England favored China anyway, and few accepted the atrocity stories until Creelman's incredible account reached the United States and appeared in the *New York World* on December 11, 1894.[58]

Creelman's revelations caused an immediate sensation and readers snapped up copies of the *World* as soon as they hit the street. Unwilling to let a good thing pass, Pulitzer's paper exploited the Port Arthur exposé and hired British war artist Frederic Villiers to forward sketches of the carnage. Villiers' prints showing piles of mutilated Chinese corpses stacked in the alleys of Port Arthur made the front page. When interest in the atrocities lagged, the yellow journal rekindled public attention by uncovering a Japanese plot to bribe Creelman if he would ignore the whole affair.[59] At the same time, House interviewed Japanese officials in Tokyo for the *World* to elicit their response to Creelman's stories. House talked with Japanese Foreign Minister Mutsu who admitted to the sympathetic correspondent that some excesses might have occurred.[60]

Creelman's articles led some to doubt their pro-Japanese sympathies, and newspapers which only days before extolled the virtues of Japan's progress and civilization now castigated the other Oriental barbarian. The outrages committed by civilized Japan seemed just as revolting as those perpetrated by heathen China, and the influence of Christian teaching and Western morality appeared "only a thin varnish, scratch it, and the barbarian is revealed." [61] According to this argument, Japan had modernized too rapidly, imitating but not understanding the conceptions of material progress and higher civilization. Suddenly Japanese, who had become tall and fair-skinned world leaders a few months before, now were called sly and evil little figures.[62]

Despite this disapprobation, Creelman's revelations actually served to strengthen sympathy for Japan, and Americans rushed to her defense, calling the atrocities a natural reaction to Chinese barbarism. Free-lance correspondent Frank G. Carpenter reminded his audience that when Japanese warriors had entered Port Arthur they had discovered archways of heads with noses and ears missing. Carpenter doubted whether highly disciplined American soldiers would act any different under similar circumstances. "After all, war is war," Colonel E. F. Gregory of the U.S. Army observed, and no one had objected to identical cases of brutality during the American Civil War, the Franco-Prussian War, or the Russo-Turkish War. "To say that the Japanese have relapsed to barbarism, or have come down to the savage level of their foes," champions of Japan concluded, "is an absurd misstatement." [63]

The Port Arthur debate prompted further favorable comparisons between the United States and Japan and focused on the two nations' identical wartime experiences. Apologists remembered that in recent times American troops had confronted similar provocation and had reacted in a remarkably analogous fashion, particularly after the Alamo massacre and the Battle of Little Big Horn. American soldiers had avenged Santa Anna's brutality in Texas and the Seventh Cavalry had butchered Indian men, women, and children near Wounded Knee Creek on the Pine Ridge Reservation to punish the murder of over 250 of their fellow troopers. The Port Arthur bloodshed was seen as just another case of justifiable reprisal again barbaric savages. [64]

The Cleveland government's examination of Creelman's charges bolstered Japan's defenders. Certain that Tokyo could explain the situation, Minister Dun called on Foreign Minister Mutsu. The Japanese leader branded Creelman's fabrications sensational, grossly exaggerated, and unjust. [65] Next, Dun interviewed a number of Western eyewitnesses of the Port Arthur operation, including American, French, and Russian military attachés. These officers had entered the Chinese stronghold with Japanese soldiers and had observed the killing. They labeled Creelman's letters a distortion of the truth and claimed he overplayed observations of wounds caused by bayonet attacks. There had been needless bloodshed, Lieutenant Michael J. O'Brien, a young infantry officer recently sent to Tokyo as American military attaché, observed, but not enough to be called a massacre. Other witnesses repeated these views. Dun collected this evidence and forwarded it, along with an overly sympathetic report which echoed Mutsu's statements to him, to Washington. "The account sent to the *World* by Mr. Creelman is sensational in the extreme and a gross exaggeration of what occurred," Dun wrote Gresham. [66]

Dun's findings and exemplary Japanese behavior after
Port Arthur, particularly in their attack on Weihaiwei,
restored American confidence in Japan. In some respects
Weihaiwei was a replica of Port Arthur with its Western-
designed fortifications, gun emplacements, dockyards, and
repair stations. The city remained the one obstacle to
Japan's domination of the sea since the Peiyang squadron
had found refuge there after the fall of Port Arthur.
Japanese commanders outlined a plan patterned on the
earlier campaign across the Gulf of Chihli, which involved
the landing of an army behind the fortress and attacking
from the rear. On January 10, 1895, scarcely more than a
month after Port Arthur, a Japanese army disembarked
below Weihaiwei. The expedition included many Port
Arthur veterans and most of the same officers involved in
the previous operation. For two weeks the Japanese advanced, storming a series of Chinese earthworks and
palisades; resistance proved stubborn, especially at the
Motienling forts, and Japanese casualties became much
heavier than they had been around Port Arthur. After a
month of fighting the Chinese surrendered Weihaiwei.[67]

The Japanese, in contrast to the Port Arthur operation,
displayed marked restraint at Weihaiwei. They released
Chinese prisoners with two days' supply of food and provided a steamer to carry the body of the Chinese naval
commander who had committed suicide and his surviving
staff back to Tientsin. American observers permitted access
to the battle area found no evidence of atrocities, although
the intensity of fighting had surpassed anything experienced
at Port Arthur. Perhaps the presence of foreigners, including
intelligence officers from the U.S. cruiser *Charleston,*
assured Japanese precautions against a repeat of the massacre. In any event Weihaiwei silenced criticism of Japanese
conduct at Port Arthur.[68]

One final aspect of actual hostilities, the work of the
Japanese Red Cross Society, completed representation of
Japan as an American protégé in East Asia. The humani-
tarian organization had been founded in 1877 as the
Society of Benevolence and had adhered to the Geneva

Convention in 1886, changing its name to the Red Cross Society of Japan the same year. In 1893 the society numbered 36,700 subscribers, but the war swelled its membership to 160,000. The imperial family and prominent leaders patronized the group and even Japanese-Americans contributed thousands of dollars during the war. Japan's Red Cross sent six physicians and twelve nurses with each troop transport bound for Korea and China, and according to the American Medical Association provided each one with the best training in medical techniques and the newest antiseptics.[69]

Unsurpassed Japanese military medicine, field hospitals, and treatment of wounded induced the United States government to borrow information from Japan. Secretary Gresham requested copies of pamphlets issued by the Medical Division of the Japanese War Department while Minister Dun forwarded samples of equipment used by the Japanese Army Medical Corps for study in Washington. The United States Navy dispatched *Charleston*'s navy surgeon C. U. Gravatt on a tour of Japanese field hospitals. Gravatt's investigation revealed a humane and modern medical corps, immaculate surgical facilities, and typhoid fever patients treated with the latest technique of "hydro-chloric acid." He observed efficient nurses busily bandaging wounds of both Japanese and Chinese casualties with bags of mercuric gauze. Gravatt marveled at the smooth organization of every unit from the dressing stations at the front down to the main field hospitals. The navy surgeon also paid particular attention to sanitary measures instituted by occupation officials who employed Chinese laborers to clean streets and houses in captured towns. "Closets have been constructed at many of the corners," Gravatt explained, "and Chinamen are fined when detected in committing nuisances." [70]

W. A. P. Martin, an American scholar and head of the Interpreters College in Peking, concurred with Gravatt's findings and added his own appraisal of Japan's medical services. Wounded and crippled Chinese prisoners, Martin wrote, returned to China in good health and with cork substitutes for their missing limbs. "When and where in our Civil War," he asked, "were prisoners provided with 'cork legs'?" [71] Reading of Japan's modern hospital system and humane treatment of wounded Chinese, Americans believed that this rather than atrocities committed in the heat of battle displayed the true spirit of the East Asian nation.[72] American missionary J. H. DeForest declared that the work of the Red Cross Society "has helped give Japan power to wage war on a higher plane of humanitarian spirit than has ever been reached before, even in Christian nations." [73] Commentary on Japanese military medicine settled the argument of Japan's status as a modern and civilized nation, and few disagreed with the American Medical Association when it concluded that "truly the Japanese is a wonderful man." [74]

Philadelphia Press. Reprinted from *Literary Digest*, April 1895.

7

Reviving Interest in East Asia

Japan had fulfilled American expectations and predictions
by demonstrating technological excellence, human courage
in battle, and the successful assimilation of Western
learning. Port Arthur increased fascination for the Japanese
and reinforced the view that in all characteristics Japanese
were just like Americans. Now that Japan's victory over
China appeared certain, war commentators sat back and
thought about what the East Asian conflict meant for the
United States. Japan's series of uninterrupted successes
over a much larger foe prompted an analysis of the Sino-
Japanese War and its broader significance for American
civilization and foreign relations. Discussions at both the
popular and scholarly levels focused on an evaluation of
Oriental cultures within the context of American conceptions of historical development, progress, and Social
Darwinism. Plagued by economic depression, social unrest,
and intellectual doubts in the United States during the
1890s, some hoped to discover solutions for their own
problems by studying the examples of virile Japan and decadent China. Others believed that Far Eastern markets
might alleviate economic and social distress in their own
country. In any event, China and Japan seemed to provide
a laboratory for testing attitudes concerning the meaning
of contemporary civilization.

Writers contrasted the traits of the combatants to explain
how 40 million people could subdue 400 million. Any
people needed a sense of national awareness to succeed,
and since China lacked this unity, it appeared doomed to
extinction. Because of its provincial diversity, senior

diplomat Charles Denby asserted, China cannot be regarded
as a viable national entity.[1] This regrettable deficiency
stemmed from China's organic evolution, military historian
and Harvard lecturer Theodore A. Dodge postulated. "The
body of China was not homogeneously sentient," Dodge
argued, "as if the nervous system of the mass was so sub-
divided that a lesion to one part did not reach the nervous
center of the whole structure." The historian claimed
further that China's bulk alone could not win a war against
organized and unified Japan any more than the Persian
hosts could defeat a Greek city-state.[2] Lucius H. Foote,
first American minister to Korea, added his own interpretation of China's impotence and found a cumbersome
bureaucracy motivated by personal aggrandizement
dominating China's densely ignorant population. This bred
an atmosphere of distrust and national apathy, Foote
stated, and he concluded that China "has always been an
enigma among nations, exclusive, anomalous and grotesque,
she seems to be a petrified relic of the past." [3]

Most Americans considered an honest and efficient central
government essential for national survival. Peking, however,
provided neither for China. Official corruption hindered
an effective war effort, venality led to one defeat after
another, and treacherous subalterns siphoned funds allo-
cated for prosecution of the war to build a magnificent stone
barge and gardens for the empress dowager. Indifferent
and politically naïve Chinese citizens, used to centuries of
subordination to authority, turned their backs on corruption.
"Piles of shells made of mud have been exhibited as the
real article," Denby informed Gresham. "Provisions have
proved worthless, high priced guns useless, regimental lists
of men have been fictitious; commanding officers have
embezzled military funds; men have gone without pay." [4]
Chinese warships passed inspection armed with huge can-
nonballs of black-painted clay, and forced coolie labor cut
wood for harbor defense booms as contractors squeezed
the government for regular wage labor.[5]

China also lacked the strong national leadership needed
for military success. No great general or minister emerged

to save China, and even old hero Li Hung-chang fell into disrepute. Li was one of the biggest boodlers in history, American Board missionary W. S. Ament charged.[6] He had started the Asian war, Denby alleged, but even if one did not believe this assertion at least the world had overestimated him. Called China's greatest statesman not many months earlier, Li Hung-chang now became the object of ridicule in the press and the subject of a popular ditty which read:

> Li Hung-chang he belly sick,
> Alle samee he get lick;
> Chinese makee muchee racket,
> Li Hung lost he yelle jacket.

> Li Hung he get licked again
> On the sea by monkey men;
> Alle samee chillee weather,
> Li Hung lose he peacock feather.

> Next time Li Hung get lick
> Better watch out belly quick;
> There'll be a pretty how-dy do,
> And Chang will lose his pigtail, too! [7]

Social Darwinists in the United States explained China's national weakness as well as its inherent corruption in terms of the biological inertness of the Chinese people. They were not exactly diseased, Dodge suggested, and many young Chinese men could play football for any American college, but even if he looked robust, the "Chinaman is filthy in mind, body, and estate." According to this Harvard scholar, the lethargic and slovenly creatures could best serve the world as mere human animals because they had less refined nervous systems than Aryans.[8] These subhuman traits supposedly made the Chinese oblivious to cuts, and they could "endure unblenched the pain of a surgical operation which would seriously compromise the reactionary power of most white men." [9] These primitive, animal-like traits were graphically illustrated to Theodore Roosevelt by Speck von Sternburg, who sent the future president sketches of Chinese infantry which clearly resembled apes with sloping foreheads and long pigtails. Sternburg knew that Roosevelt, then police commissioner in New York City, had studied the impact of gunshot wounds on the human body by having his men test their revolvers on corpses. He thought his American comrade would be interested to learn that he had also studied pistol wounds on Chinese soldiers who had just walked 320 miles over the Liaotung Peninsula and had survived. "What fighting material you could make out of those chaps!" Sternburg concluded.[10]

Few Americans in 1894 denied that a moral and religious people made a strong nation. China's disintegration could be explained by its reliance on heathen superstitions and cruel, immoral habits. Chinese soldiers reportedly looked to war gods and green dragons rather than powder and lead to defeat their enemies and carried umbrellas, fans, and ceremonial chickens into combat, not modern rifles and mess kits. Ignorant villagers refused to dig wells for sanitary conditions in their towns because they feared the holes would puncture the earth and disturb departed ancestors. Americans read that infanticide and other horrible practices existed on a large scale in China and heard about rewards offered for Japanese heads. The Chinese emperor was supposed to be an effeminate, depraved individual, served by 10,000 eunuchs, who made his subjects and foreign dignitaries crawl like reptiles (kowtow) to the foot of the throne to seek interviews.[11]

Revelations of China's internal imperfections stigmatized the country's wartime identity, but the unhealthy influence on the rest of East Asia deserved even greater condemnation. China threatened the genius of progress in the area, Durham White Stevens, an American secretary employed by the Japanese legation in Washington, insisted, and he found China's hand in the Korean domestic dissension which led to Sino-Japanese war. "Her influence is secret, but none the less patent," Stevens contended. "She shirks responsibility to other nations, but hesitates at no means—cajolery, bribery, menace—to dominate Korea."[12] Howard

Martin, a former secretary in the American legation at Peking, supported Stevens' self-serving arguments. The United States had a special interest in the outcome of the struggle over Korea, he wrote, since Americans had opened the Hermit Kingdom to Western contact and the government and public had obligations to oppose China's policy of enslavement. The war pitted Japanese progress against Chinese extermination, Martin concluded.[13]

Seeking dramatic contrasts to explain Japan's triumph, writers and journalists developed the theme of progressive, reformist, and modern Japan opening the Far East to commerce and Christianity. According to this often repeated concept, the Japanese had adapted gracefully to modernization, had adopted Western technology, and had assimilated Western learning. The same ideals that made the United States a great and powerful nation ensured Japan an equal place in the world. Supposedly Japanese exemplified Christian virtue by their honesty, amiability, loyalty, filial piety, and law-abiding steadiness. In fact, they had learned to respect law even more than the Anglo-Saxons and had matched Americans in courage and tenacity and despite their diminutive size displayed a physical stamina unsurpassed in all the world.[14]

Essayists like Lucius Foote, Lafcadio Hearn, and others returned to earlier theories and predicted that before long the Japanese body would grow to Anglo-Saxon proportions to keep pace with its Westernized mind. Once again the Japanese became close kin to the white man. "While the Japanese are dark skinned there is no race prejudice against them in other countries," an Atlanta, Georgia, editor remarked during the war, "and they are cordially received in circles where a Chinaman or an East Indian would be barred." Learning that Japan's young prince searched for a wife among European royalty, this same southern scribe suggested that an American girl would make an admirable empress of Japan.[15] The theme of Japanese as "Yankees of the Orient" reappeared as the Asians pushed their warfare against China in a businesslike, practical, and peculiarly American manner.[16]

Though predominantly pro-Japanese, public discussion of the war and its relation to American foreign policy included a few dissenting voices. Critics warned against Japan's imperialistic ambitions in the Far East, the Pacific Ocean, and Hawaii. Some even foresaw a future Japanese-American economic and military rivalry in the area. In a sermon delivered in October 1894 at New York City's Calvary Church, the Reverend Robert MacArthur begged the United States to strengthen its fleet in East Asian seas as a precaution against Japanese expansion. Reviewing the sermon, the editor of a West Coast commercial magazine cautioned that unless the United States occupied Pearl Harbor permanently one day the Japanese would seize it. The Sino-Japanese War revealed the need for a larger fleet, the construction of an interoceanic canal in Central America, and full participation in Asian affairs.[17]

Former minister to Korea Augustine Heard, a Boston merchant interested in American investment in the Far East, warned that unless his government became more active in East Asia Japan would drive it out of the entire region and close the door to the China market. Japan aimed at a total monopoly of Korean transportation, fishing industry, and gold mines, Heard claimed. He disagreed with those who blamed China for starting the war and pointed out that traditionally Koreans had adopted Chinese culture and respected their tributary master's ideas and institutions while despising the selfish Japanese. "If Korea falls into the hands of Japan," he concluded, "God help her!" [18] State Department Asian expert W. W. Rockhill shared Heard's evaluation of Japan and, though predicting that a good thrashing of China would be "the only tonic which seems to suit that queer country," feared Japan's smashing victories. "The Lord only knows where they will stop," he wrote a friend in China.[19]

American religious workers and peace advocates also criticized Japan. Missionaries residing in Japan, losing prestige and position to dynamic Japanese Christians, reproved Japan's steady penetration of mainland Asia and series of war gains. The Reverend Dwight Learned observed from Kyoto how Japan had humbled a great power, once considered indestructible by England and France, and had discovered a heaven-given mission to free China and the rest of Asia from the control of the Western world. Learned found the common people behaving rudely toward Americans and demanding that they leave Japan at once.[20] The American Peace Society also censured Japan and noted that the Asian power had marched to civilization through seas of blood while ignoring corresponding moral and religious developments. The peace group qualified its condemnation of Japan, blaming instead Western, Christian powers for supplying Asians with modern weapons and teaching them the art of contemporary warfare.[21]

Though some questioned Japan's motives, the depiction of Japan as a reformist and civilizing nation intent upon establishing a stable international structure in the Far East persisted and won widespread acceptance in the United States. Exponents of the Japanese cause urged the United States government to abandon neutrality and support the crusade to modernize the rest of Eastern Asia. Former missionary William Elliot Griffis, considered one of the foremost Asian experts in the 1890s, became an ardent and vocal advocate of close Japanese-American ties. The fifty-one-year-old author of the best-selling *Mikado's Empire* had gone to Japan in 1871, had founded a scientific school in Echizen, and later had taught organic chemistry at the Imperial University in Tokyo, where he had observed the influence of Western education on Japan. He expected Japan, aided by active sympathy in America, to transmit this learning to the rest of Asia. "Let us hope that true Americanism and the work of our nation will be that of the Great Pacific Power," Griffis stated. That task could begin at once by helping Japan in the war against China, since the contest marked another chapter in man's struggle against slavery, absolutism, barbarism, and tyranny.[22]

While many students of the war delighted at the prospect of a Japanese victory which would force reform on China, they desired American rather than Japanese direction of postwar reconstruction. People in Shanghai assumed the

United States would furnish manpower and supplies to rebuild devastated China and develop an extensive system of internal improvement, Consul General Jernigan remarked to the State Department. Consul Read presented an identical impression from Tientsin. "It will be my aim that America whose hands are clean as regards China, shall secure her fair share of the orders to be placed, and shall come forward as the best country from which to draw men and material." [23] Back in Washington, Rockhill also hoped the war would lead to increased investment in China, but he feared it meant instead the beginning of a Japanese-American rivalry in the Far East since Japan possessed advanced machinery, inventive genius, and cheap labor to undersell American traders in East Asian markets. Japan's own vigorous search for commercial outlets, Rockhill observed, blocked projects and investments and hindered penetration of the China market.[24]

The Asian marketplace did not particularly interest the present administration in Washington, and President Cleveland and Secretary Gresham did not listen to Rockhill's warnings about future Japanese estrangement. In fact, after months of pro-Japanese agitation in the press and in public statments by a variety of war commentators, the two leaders seemed ready to support Japan. The president openly praised the island nation and told Congress "the Japanese Empire of today is no longer the Japan of the past and our relations with this progressive nation should not be less broad and liberal than those with other powers." He lauded Japan's desire for "more liberal intercourse, complete autonomy in her domestic affairs, and full equality in the family of nations." [25] Gresham, while publicly defending the administration's policy of strict neutrality, admitted to Dun in Tokyo that he had long sympathized with Japan, the most civilized country in Asia. "Japan has stepped out into the light of a better day," the secretary confided to Senator Morgan, "and she regards the United States as her best friend." [26]

Although Gresham did not as yet discard American

neutrality, his pro-Japanese propensity probably influenced his approach to the question of treaty revisions with China and Japan. Both nations pressed for treaty revision in 1894. China wanted a formal pact which defined immigration laws and the status of Chinese-Americans. Japan insisted upon the removal of all vestiges of the early unequal treaties between the United States and Japan such as extraterritorial jurisdiction. The question of treaty relations with China centered on immigration. Nationwide anti-Chinese prejudice contributed to the movement for complete restriction of Chinese immigrants as well as the registration or deportation of aliens already in the United States. As the American Federation of Labor argued in May 1894, "It is needless here to discuss the impossibility of the amalgamation or assimilation of the Chinese in America with our people." The Sino-Japanese War increased such sentiment, for there were fears that Japanese conquests might drive defeated Chinese to seek refuge in the United States. We don't want these "dirty folks" to flee to California shores, exclusionists stated, and they demanded immigration laws to protect the country from having homeless Orientals dumped on it.[27]

Already in March 1894 Gresham and Yang Ju had signed a convention enumerating such restrictions, and in August President Cleveland had ratified it. The Gresham-Yang Treaty prohibited further immigration to the United States for a period of ten years and clarified questions left vague in an earlier pact signed in 1880. The 1894 arrangement was far more restrictive than the original Sino-American Immigration Treaty of November 17, 1880, in which Article I had provided that the United States government might "regulate, limit, or suspend" Chinese immigration "but may not absolutely prohibit it." Article I of the new treaty, however, prescribed that immigration of Chinese laborers "shall be absolutely prohibited." In September the Gresham-Yang document arrived in China for approval; and Gresham worried about war-induced public utterances against China, believing these detrimental to acceptance of the restrictive covenant. China was in no position to argue, though, and signed the treaty which was clearly an affront to her.[28]

While Gresham discussed treaty relations with China, both Japanese Minister Tateno and his successor Kurino flooded the State Department with requests for a new treaty of their own. Tateno had never been successful in settling treaty differences, but Kurino, speaking often of current sympathy for Japan and of his nation's military successes, became bolder and pressed harder for a revision favorable to Japan.[29] Whitelaw Reid, for one, hoped Kurino, whom he called the triumphant Asiatic heathen, would force Gresham to revise the existing Japanese-American treaty. "We have not behaved well to Japan in the matter of the new treaty, and I fancy that now since they have got their treaty through with Great Britain and have made such a military success, they are feeling a little more like taking a strong tone with Mr. Gresham." [30] The British government, Reid wrote, already had outwitted Gresham by promising that the British would wait until the United States had negotiated a new pact with Japan before concluding a similar arrangement. But while Gresham wavered, Great Britain had gone ahead and abandoned its extraterritorial rights and had recognized Japan as an equal partner in East Asia. The sluggish-minded secretary of state, a Reid editorial concluded, had embarrassed the United States by ignoring Japan's request for treaty revision while a former critic of the Asian nation had concluded a friendly pact.[31]

Gresham had every intention of negotiating a new treaty with Japan, and on November 23, 1894, Kurino and Gresham signed a pact which abolished American consular jurisdiction over the affairs of its citizens in Japan and provided for more equitable commercial relations. Japan considered this removal of extraterritorial privilege more important than all her victories against China, one journalist commented, and the acceptance of the treaty by the Senate would assure her an equal place among the most advanced nations.[32] No one could misinterpret the meaning of the two treaties of 1894. One offered a humiliating slap to China; the other a bow to Japanese prestige.

Another treaty, that concluded at Shimonoseki in April 1895 ending the Sino-Japanese War, prompted further analysis of the conflict's significance for the United States. The Treaty of Shimonoseki was signed on April 17, and the details of the pact reached Washington on April 25. It provided for Korean independence, cession of territory on the Liaotung Peninsula, surrender of Formosa and the Pescadores, the payment of a $150 million indemnity, and the opening of treaty ports to heavy machinery imports and foreign manufactures.[33]

American diplomats in East Asia commented extensively on the final arrangements. Usually reticent Edwin Dun forwarded a rambling, philosophical dispatch to the State Department describing how the war had changed conditions in China and Japan which would have a far reaching impact on American diplomacy in the region. Dun's colleague in China, Charles Denby, sent a brooding message to Gresham which discussed the long-range implications of China's surrender to what he felt were unusually harsh and punitive terms. Denby charged that Japan's seizure of territory made her a continental power and would upset the status quo in East Asia and force European intervention. The United States, he concluded, should use its influence to moderate Japanese policies.[34]

While Denby revealed his forebodings to his government, European statesmen planned to intervene in the settlement of the Sino-Japanese War. German undersecretary of state for foreign affairs Max von Brandt, a former minister to China and acquaintance of Li Hung-chang, and Russian minister in Peking Count Arturo P. Cassini coordinated efforts to block Japan's seizure of Chinese continental territory. Though rebuffed by Great Britain, Cassini and von Brandt gained the approval of France for a tripartite understanding to check Japanese expansion. On April 17, immediately after the signature of the peace treaty, Russia requested the support of Berlin and Paris in a "friendly demarche," advising Japan to refrain from the occupation of any mainland property. Ministers of the three powers delivered their verbal and confidential admonitions to the Japanese Foreign Office in Tokyo. Japanese presence on the Liaotung Peninsula rendered the independence of Korea "illusory," they insisted, and disturbed future peace in the Far East. If Japan refused to give up its new territories, the Russian representative revealed, the trio might use sea power to isolate the Japanese armies in China.[35]

The tripartite intervention evoked little surprise in the United States. Both the government and press had expected it during the course of the war, and the desire to prevent such interference in the Asian war had been one motive behind increased interest in the distant conflict and a factor in the decision to offer good offices to end the war and other measures designed to limit fighting and tensions in Korea and China. On several occasions Gresham had warned Japan to limit its demands so as not to bring about European reprisals. Cleveland and Gresham had decided to send troops to Peking to protect missionaries and to offset European influence, not because they wanted any territorial or economic concessions. The administration had been forced to take a more active interest by its self-defined role as an example of antiimperialism among the scrambling and greedy European nations. "Not a great while before the treaty of peace between China and Japan," Gresham's wife remembered, "I heard my husband tell Senator Platt of Connecticut that he feared Russia, France, England, and Germany, in the event of the Japanese armies crushing China, might, under the guise of preserving order in China, partition that country."[36]

American diplomats in East Asia also cautioned against European aggression unleashed by the Sino-Japanese War. In March 1895, Denby wrote Gresham to keep his eye on Russia as the power most likely to disturb the future peace. He maintained that Great Britain and even Japan as satisfied countries in Asia would cooperate with the United States to preserve peace and stability in this critical region.[37] Minister Sill in Seoul issued similar warnings and declared that the Korean king hoped to use Russia to oust the Japanese conquerors from his country.[38] A Russo-Japanese war appeared probable, Consul General Jernigan explained from Shanghai, and would plunge East Asia into anarchy, scrambles for concessions, and the establishment of permanent spheres of influence which would close China to Americans.[39] Others, including Consul Read and legation secretary Horace Allen, expected further conflict, though Allen wanted Russia to attack Japan and expressed excitement at the prospect of observing "the chip knocked off the shoulder of the cheeky little Jap." [40]

Few shared Allen's opinion and most interested Americans hoped for Japanese diplomatic triumphs over the three greedy European powers. Even John Foster now worked for speedy Chinese capitulation to Japan's treaty demands, and when he learned that the Russian, French, and German agents in Peking had exerted influence in the imperial court to prevent ratification of the peace pact, he urged Li Hung-chang to journey to the capital and defend the Treaty of Shimonoseki. Li insisted that his many enemies dominated Peking and Foster would be a more effective envoy to explain the terms to China's leaders. After some hesitation, the former U.S. secretary of state consented and left for the Chinese imperial city.[41] Once in Peking, Foster accepted advice from Li's friends and discarded his interpreter in favor of one "cheerfully" supplied by Denby and the American legation. He also established headquarters in the American compound. Therefore, when Foster traveled to his interview with the imperial cabinet, containing the ten most influential men in the empire, his mission appeared officially sanctioned by the United States government rather than by Li Hung-chang. The dignified former secretary argued for ratification in front of Chinese and Manchu bureaucrats and reminded them that the treaty was not Li's personal affair but the emperor's because the peace mission had been sent under imperial rescript. The emperor's advisers listened carefully and may have been swayed by his arguments since they petitioned their monarch to sign the treaty.[42]

Japanese policies also contributed to the cabinet's decision. Cognizant that continued procrastination strengthened
the tripartite position, Japan refused China's request for
a ten-day delay in ratifications. The Japanese government
ordered immediate compliance with treaty directives, Denby
cabled Washington on May 4 ,1895, and several days later
Dun made a similar observation from Tokyo.[43] Japan
assumed this hard line with China because it had reached
an understanding with the European powers which promised
surrender of claims to the Liaotung Peninsula, except Port
Arthur and Talienwan, in return for a larger indemnity.
The Russian, French, and German ministers in Peking,
having Japan's assurances and increasingly divided over
the purpose of the three-power pact, instructed China to
exchange ratifications.[44]

The Japanese peace delegation proceeded to Chefoo on
May 6 to conclude the final convention with Chinese
plenipotentiaries. But even now, bolstered by the presence
of eleven Russian warships in Chefoo harbor, China stalled.
Again Americans stepped in to facilitate communications.
Consul Read and the officers of the American gunboat
Machias, then anchored in the harbor, greeted the Japanese
delegation and forwarded their credentials to the Chinese
envoys. Messengers from the American consulate (Tientsin
served as the consular post for Chefoo) raced back and
forth between the two proud peace commissions for several
days and kept conversations going. Finally China and
Japan completed all treaty formalities and brought to an
end nine months of war.[45]

Americans in Eastern Asia breathed a sigh of relief and
commended Japan for its moderation. American Board
missionary Develло Sheffield praised Japan's restraint, while
Consul General Jernigan declared that Japan's ability to
compromise had prevented a general Asian war.[46] Japanese
flexibility in the final stages of negotiation pleased Americans because no other Western nation had contributed as
much to peace preliminaries and treaty discussions. Diplomatic representatives empowered by their government to
offer good offices had served technically as messengers

rather than mediators and they had not guided final arrangements; but both East Asian powers used American officials and private citizens to represent their own interests, and diplomats on the scene had enlarged upon their messengerial role by acting as advisers.

Japan acknowledged months of pro-Japanese attitudes and policies in the United States and expressed gratitude. It was most satisfying to read statements such as that delivered by a Japanese official at the Chefoo ratification conference who praised the American response to the war. "People of both China and Japan very highly appreciate the service done by the U.S. government, and also the part played by Mr. Foster. The American friendship to us has been consistent ever since its commencement, and our appreciation for same is daily increasing." [47] Even the Japanese emperor sent his official thanks to President Cleveland for American policies during the Sino-Japanese War which had "served to draw still closer the bonds of friendship and good neighborhood which happily united our two countries." [48]

No one at the time thought to thank Secretary of State Gresham for his efforts to restore peace in the Far East and for his long hours spent in trying to formulate a just, impartial, and humane policy toward the Sino-Japanese confrontation. For almost a year Gresham had devoted considerable time and energy to East Asian problems and had suffered daily invective from opponents of his policies. Gresham, a stubborn man certain of the correctness of his idealistic interpretation of American foreign policies, never understood why his legalistic-moralistic motives drew such ugly criticism. He expected some partisan reaction to his abandonment of former colleagues but never the bitterness which accompanied attacks on his diplomacy and on his character. The sixty-three-year-old official had worked hard to construct an unimpeachable and untainted diplomacy, and when even this had been questioned, he became overly sensitive to all forms of opposition. He grew tired and his health suffered. In late April 1895 Gresham caught a cold, it developed into pneumonia, and on May

28 he died. The secretary was concentrating on the Anglo-Venezuelan boundary dispute at the time of his death, but the frustrations of the Sino-Japanese War may have already weakened his resistance to disease. Only after his demise did the Japanese government honor the secretary for his honest and just diplomacy. Minister Kurino visited Gresham's widow and presented a lovely tapestry and two exquisite cloisonné vases from the emperor of Japan as a token of his country's affection for the late secretary of state.[49]

The secretary's untimely death deeply affected his close friends Cleveland, Carlisle, and Civil War comrades. Most Americans, however, noted his passing almost casually. He had apparently been a mediocre statesman and few mourned him. His many Republican enemies, in fact, hardly tempered their judgment of Gresham as the years went by. This biased impression came to dominate later views of Gresham, and generations of historians brushed him aside as one of the least effective individuals ever to direct the State Department. Gresham, it seemed, contributed absolutely nothing to the record of American diplomacy.[50]

Gresham did not rank with John Quincy Adams, William Seward, or Hamilton Fish as a major architect of nine-teenth-century foreign policies, but neither was he a non-entity in the State Department. During the Sino-Japanese War of 1894–1895, he made some positive decisions and suggested other policies which would have a lasting impact on the direction and goals of American diplomacy in East Asia. He reinforced the policy of strict neutrality toward Far Eastern conflicts introduced by earlier administrations, strengthened the traditional good offices service, and added new emphasis to America's self-imposed obligation to preserve peace and order in unstable areas far from the Western Hemisphere. This approach entangled the United States in East Asian problems and prompted the sending of troops and warships to uphold this concept. Gresham accepted the added responsibilities even though they might lead to the type of expansion he deplored. The secretary defined positive duties of American neutrality in Asian wars,

where the United States must offer good offices to restore
order while protecting its own citizens and maritime rights.
All these issues had been confronted before, but perhaps
not quite so intensely in response to Far Eastern problems,
and some of these same burdens would be faced again
and in a remarkably similar manner by another legalistic-
moralistic administration under Woodrow Wilson.

Gresham's diplomacy was one of many precedents not
only for Wilsonian conduct from 1914 to 1917 but ironically also for his foremost Republican critics when they
regained control of foreign policy in 1896. Gresham-
Cleveland diplomacy in East Asia during the Korean
insurrection and the Sino-Japanese War provided part of
the pattern for over a decade of American policies in the
Far East. Presidents William McKinley and Theodore
Roosevelt followed essentially the same approach toward
China, Japan, and Korea suggested by Gresham and Cleveland. There was no dramatic new Asian policy appearing
suddenly when Americans acquired the Philippines after
the Spanish-American War of 1898 or even when Secretary
of State John Hay circulated the Open Door Notes in 1899
and 1900. American military intervention in the Boxer
Rebellion in 1900 comprised no dramatic new strategy.
In fact, there appears to be a notable continuity between
what Gresham and Cleveland understood to be American
duties in the Far East and the McKinley and Theodore
Roosevelt administrations' conduct in the same area. They
all promoted Japanese-American friendship as a counter-
balance to European imperialism, good offices to preserve
peace and stability, and the dispatch of military forces to
help keep order.

Roosevelt's arbitral responsibilities during the Russo-
Japanese War of 1904–1905, though more successful than
similar functions during the Sino-Japanese War, differed
little in principle from Gresham's and Cleveland's approach
during the earlier Asian crisis. In 1894 the president even
indicated that the warring nations might meet in the United
States to end the fighting, as Russia and Japan would later
do at Portsmouth, New Hampshire, by Roosevelt's invi-

tation. Gresham's good offices program and Denby-Dun intermediation can be viewed in a like manner. The goal of mediation and friendship toward both belligerents centered on the desire to check a bloody scramble for concessions in disintegrating Imperial China. The breakup of China into spheres of influence would upset the traditional policy of equal commercial, missionary, and diplomatic opportunities. Cleveland and Gresham never enunciated a clear open door policy or program of commercial promotion, but they strengthened the open door principal by insisting that an equal American force should be available to guard U.S. interests in Peking and Seoul. The commitment of military personnel to mainland Asia was not a policy alternative employed only after the Spanish-American War had brought large numbers of U.S. troops and warships to the Far East. The deployment of a considerable force in Peking during the Boxer Rebellion was simplified by occupation of the Philippines, but Cleveland and Gresham accepted an identical solution to East Asian problems during the Sino-Japanese War, and with far less actual military power. They had landed marines in Korea and in China, they had concentrated eight warships in Asian waters, and they had given Denby permission to call troops to Peking. Cleveland and Gresham were fortunate that anti-Western sentiment had not crystallized sufficiently in late 1894 to necessitate the protection of the Peking legation.

Admittedly a facile comparison of Gresham-Cleveland diplomacy in East Asia with that of McKinley and Roosevelt oversimplifies a complex question of American-East Asian relations, as well as ignoring fundamental differences in their philosophies of foreign relations and the domestic pressures on the different administrations. But in 1894 and 1895 the United States government formulated and applied definite policies to Far Eastern problems, and the McKinley and Roosevelt administrations developed these conceptions more fully and pursued them more forcefully and positively. Why then have the second Cleveland government's contributions to late nineteenth-century East Asian diplomacy been obscured by the later experiences?

While John Hay's programs have been termed sound and successful and Theodore Roosevelt's have been called shrewd, skillful, and responsible, the Gresham-Cleveland diplomacy in the same area has been considered of little or no importance. In fact, very few American diplomatic histories or studies of the Cleveland years even mention that Gresham and Cleveland had an Asian policy.

Disregard of Gresham-Cleveland diplomacy in the Far East stems partly from the two statesmen's conduct. The president never maintained a constant interest in East Asia, focusing only occasionally on the remote diplomatic controversy. He considered domestic problems and Latin American issues far more important for the United States government and the American people. Nevertheless during the Korean rebellion he offered mediation and unsuccessful in that direction next ordered Sill to do everything possible to prevent an Asian war. Later in the Sino-Japanese dispute Cleveland debated the dispatch of marines to Peking. More often, though, he ignored Asian politics and let his loyal secretary bear the brunt of partisan and public criticism of a highly unpopular neutrality and frustrating good offices policy. For his part, Gresham clothed his own contributions in legalisms and moral judgments. He understood that American interests required peace and order in China and Korea and supported a program of equal opportunities for all nations in the region, but the U.S. government could not actively promote these interests. He offered good offices and considered the utilization of American soldiers to defend both Chinese and Japanese citizens and property as well as for the protection of missionaries. At the same time, though, Gresham warned his diplomats to remain strictly neutral while pursuing these objectives and cautioned other Americans to avoid any involvement in the war, resisting public and private efforts to increase influence in East Asia by exploiting the opportunities afforded by the Asian power struggle. Thus, both Cleveland's and Gresham's approach to the Far East appeared negative and contradictory while in reality they outlined policies and set certain precedents.

Public attitudes during this same period were far more precise and definable. Many watchful Americans discussed the Korean troubles and Sino-Japanese War. Religious workers, journalists, businessmen, labor spokesmen, scholars, and diplomats contributed to what might be called a public opinion about the Asian crisis of 1894–1895. This opinion supported Japan. Informed observers predicted from the beginning of the struggle that Japan would win in its fight with China. They considered Japan the stabilizing element in Eastern Asia and a bulwark against European efforts to partition China. Japan became the power most likely to defend equal opportunities for trade, travel, and missionary endeavors in the Far East. Accordingly, Japan served American interests in that remote part of the world. The lengths to which some identified with the island empire became ludicrous as they called Japanese the Yankees of the Orient, American protégés, and good friends. Japan's victory seemed a triumph of American civilization and would expand the Asian marketplace, alleviating over-production and domestic unrest in the United States. Japanese conquests would open China and Korea to Christianity, American manufactured goods, and Western education. Dissenters from this view comprised a decided minority.

War commentators assumed that American neutrality weakened Japan's resistance to European pressure and prolonged Chinese diplomatic efforts to isolate Japan. However there was no organized or concerted public cam-paign pressing the United States government to support Japan, though constant pro-Japanese sentiment may have caused the administration to view Japan more favorably and bend a little in her direction. Discussions about the war were scattered and impressionistic, and most politicians and prominent Americans did not mention the conflict in their correspondence. Even Grover Cleveland said little privately about the war. Lodge, Theodore Roosevelt, Reid, and of course active diplomats were exceptions. Naval personnel and missionaries also talked about the war as an immediate and personal experience. The most vocal observers, however, were journalists and editors.

Newspapers devoted substantial space to the Sino-Japanese struggle. A survey of large-circulation dailies across the United States revealed complete war coverage. Papers in the Northeast, South, Midwest, and Far West ran front-page articles on the more sensational events. The Korean insurrection, Yalu battle, Port Arthur massacre, and Shimonoseki peace talks all earned weeks of page-one headlines, pushing European, Latin American, and even domestic news off the front page. During peak war interest, at least one editorial analysis appeared each day. A cursory appraisal of smaller papers and select local sheets reinforced this observation.

Why did the war receive so much publicity when it clearly posed no threat to the United States? The mysterious Orient made good copy and offered the public a diversion from incessant headlines on unemployment, strikes, suicides, and bankruptcies in the depression-plagued nineties. Pulitzer's *New York World* exploited the sensational aspects of the war and found a ready audience for its budding yellow journalism. Whitelaw Reid's *New York Tribune* focused on the East Asian diplomacy to discredit Gresham and the Democrats. Southern papers talked about the war as a stimulus to open East Asian markets to surplus cotton. West Coast journals had obvious reasons for interest in the war, including many Asian-American residents, relative proximity to the war zone, and a growing interest in Hawaii and the Pacific Ocean. The apparent imbalance of newspaper sources in this study merely reflected contemporary American reaction to the war. It was a journalist's delight and a prelude to the sensational journalism of the Spanish-American War.

Just how important is the American response to the Sino-Japanese War for the student of American history? The war was after all a minor incident in late nineteenth-century diplomacy and politics. Yet discussion of and involvement in the conflict stimulated public interest in Eastern Asia which had been largely dormant for several years. It may have contributed to an expansionist mood, which would be expressed more clearly with the acquisition of the Philippines. The United States government within a short nine-month span further defined its commitments to that area of the world. What emerged was evidence that the country was still too weak to pursue an independent and forceful Far Eastern policy. Those who called for a larger navy noted the insignificant, though active, American squadron taxed to its capacity. The United States still relied on other nations to protect its interests; earlier it had depended on Great Britain and France, now it turned to an Americanized Japan. But there were clear signs in 1894 and 1895 that the United States would have to make its own way in East Asia. It was willing to assume larger and more complex responsibilities in order to uphold the position of impartial arbiter and friend of all nations, intent only on keeping peace and stability while quietly trading and traveling on the Asian mainland. In the final analysis, then, a study of the United States and the Sino-Japanese War of 1894–1895 documents how an idealistic administration, pressed by a critical public and caught by its own conceptions of moral and legal duties, can entangle the United States just as deeply in a foreign war as any expansionist government guided by motives of power and self-interest.

Notes

1. Cleveland, Gresham, and East Asia

1. Matilda Gresham, *Life of Walter Quintin Gresham, 1832–1895*, 2 vols. (Chicago: Rand McNally, 1919), 2: 798.

2. *Papers Relating to the Foreign Relations of the United States, 1893* (Washington: Government Printing Office, 1894), p. v, hereafter cited as *F.R.U.S.*

3. George F. Parker, ed., *The Writings and Speeches of Grover Cleveland* (New York: Cassell, 1892), p. 35; also, Caroline Thomas Harnsberger, ed., *Treasury of Presidential Quotations* (Chicago: Follett, 1964), p. 93. For an excellent discussion of Cleveland's idealistic diplomacy, see John A. S. Grenville and George Berkeley Young, *Politics, Strategy, and American Diplomacy: Studies in Foreign Policy, 1873–1917* (New Haven and London: Yale University Press, 1966), pp. 102–118; George Roscoe Dulebohm, *Principles of Foreign Policy under the Cleveland Administrations* (Philadelphia: University of Pennsylvania Press, 1941).

4. See Gresham, *Gresham;* Montgomery Schuyler, "Walter Quintin Gresham," in *The American Secretaries of State and Their Diplomacy,* ed. Samuel Flagg Bemis (New York: Knopf, 1928), 8; 227–269; *Dictionary of American Biography,* VII: 607–609.

5. Gresham, *Gresham,* 2: 670, 673.

6. Gresham to Medill, Nov. 7, 1892, quoted in ibid., p. 676.

7. Cleveland to Gresham, Jan. 25, 1893, quoted in ibid., p. 679.

8. Gresham to Cleveland, Feb. 7, 1893, quoted in ibid., pp. 682–683.

9. Gresham, quoted in ibid., p. 797.

10. Gresham to Hon. John Overmeyer, July 25, 1894, letterbook, vol. 48, Gresham Papers, Library of Congress.

11. See William Adam Russ, *The Hawaiian Revolution, 1893–94* (Selinsgrove: Susquehanna University Press, 1959).

12. *F.R.U.S., 1893,* p. xi.

13. "Typescript of Walter Q. Gresham Mem. for Mr. Parker by L. T. Michener," Michener Papers, Library of Congress; also, Grenville and Young, *Politics,* pp. 110–111.

14. Grenville and Young, *Politics,* p. 103.

15. *Register of the Department of State, Corrected to July 1, 1893* (Washington: Government Printing Office, 1893), pp. 9–15; *Re-*

port of the Secretary of the Navy; Being Part of the Messages and Documents Communicated to the Two Houses of Congress at the Beginning of the First Session of the Fifty-Fourth Congress (Washington: Government Printing Office, 1895), p. xiii; Graham H. Stuart, *The Department of State: A History of Its Organization, Procedure, and Personnel* (New York: Macmillan, 1949), pp. 180–184.

16. *Dictionary of American Biography*, 1: 105.

17. See Paul A. Varg, *Open Door Diplomat: The Life of W. W. Rockhill*, Illinois Studies in the Social Sciences, vol. 33 (Urbana: University of Illinois Press, 1952).

18. Gresham to Bayard, July 22, 1894, Gresham Papers.

19. Charles Denby, *China and Her People* (Boston: L. C. Page, 1906), 1: v, ix; John William Cassey, "The Mission of Charles Denby and International Rivalries in the Far East, 1885–1898" (Ph.D. dissertation, University of Southern California, 1959); *Dictionary of American Biography*, 5: 233–234.

20. Criticism of Denby Jr., in Cheshire to Rockhill, June 16 and Nov. 14, 1894, Rockhill Papers, Houghton Library, Harvard University; Gresham to D. Howard, Nov. 26, 1894, Gresham Papers; *Springfield Republican*, Sept. 6, 1894.

21. Foster Rhea Dulles, *Yankee and Samurai: America's Role in the Emergence of Modern Japan, 1791–1960* (New York: Harper & Row, 1965), pp. 178–179; Payson J. Treat, *Diplomatic Relations between the United States and Japan, 1853–1895*, 3 vols. (Gloucester: Peter Smith, 1963, reprint of 1932 Stanford University Press edition), 3: 25–26.

22. For the view that Allen dominated Sill, see Horace N. Allen, "Korean Collection," New York Public Library; Fred Harvey Harrington, *God, Mammon, and the Japanese: Horace N. Allen and Korean-American Relations, 1884–1905* (Madison: University of Wisconsin Press, 1944). Shirley W. Smith argues that Sill followed an independent course in Korea, in "John M. B. Sill," in *Michigan and the Cleveland Era: Sketches of University of Michigan Staff Members and Alumni Who Served the Cleveland Administrations, 1885–89, 1893–97*, ed. Earl D. Babst and Lewis Vander Velde (Ann Arbor: University of Michigan Press, 1948), p. 230.

23. Allan Nevins, *Grover Cleveland: A Study in Courage* (New York: Dodd, Mead, 1966), p. 516.

24. Letters of recommendation, in Applications and Recommendations for Public Office, 1893–1924, National Archives Record Group 59; reports of financial activities, in Despatches from United States Consuls in Tientsin, 1868–1906, vols. 4–6, National Archives Record Group 59, hereafter cited as Consul Tientsin.

25. James Harrison Wilson, *China, Travels and Investigations in*

the "Middle Kingdom" (New York: Appleton, 1887), pp. 20–21; also see Robert McClellan, *The Heathen Chinee: A Study of American Attitudes toward Chinese, 1890–1905* (Columbus: Ohio State University Press, 1971); Stuart Creighton Miller, *The Unwelcome Immigrant: The American Image of the Chinese, 1785–1882* (Berkeley and Los Angeles: University of California Press, 1969); John Berdan Gardner, "The Image of the Chinese in the United States, 1885–1915" (Ph.D. dissertation, University of Pennsylvania, 1961).

26. *Atlanta Constitution*, Aug. 5, Sept. 2 and 5, 1894. Similar views expressed in *New York Tribune*, July 2, 1894; *Pacific Commercial Advertiser*, July 17, 1894; *Boston Daily Globe*, July 23, 1894.

27. See Hilary Conroy, *The Japanese Seizure of Korea, 1868–1910* (Philadelphia: University of Pennsylvania Press, 1960), pp. 232–235; Seiji G. Hishida, *The International Position of Japan as a Great Power,* Studies in History, Economics, and Public Law, vol. 24 (New York: Columbia University Press, 1905), pp. 167–169; Arthur Judson Brown, *The Mastery of the Far East* (New York: Charles Scribner's Sons, 1919), pp. 120ff.

28. Reports of Japanese domestic problems, in Dun to Gresham, Jan. 4, 1894, Feb. 19, 1894, May 24, 1894, Despatches from United States Ministers to Japan, vol. 66, National Archives Record Group 59, hereafter cited as Japan Despatches; also see George N. Curzon, *Problems of the Far East: Japan-Korea-China* (London: Longmans, Green, 1894), pp. 33–37.

29. Kim's murder, in Dun to Gresham, Apr. 20, 1894, Japan Despatches, vol. 66; *North China Herald* 52 (Mar. 30, 1894): 470, 488; Tateno to Gresham, Apr. 5, 1894, Notes from the Japanese Legation in the United States to the Department of State, vol. 5, National Archives Record Group 59, hereafter cited as Notes from Japan; Denby Jr. to Gresham, Sept. 27, 1894, Despatches from United States Ministers to China, vol. 96, National Archives Record Group 59, hereafter cited as China Despatches.

30. See C. I. Eugene Kim and Han-kyo Kim, *Korea and the Politics of Imperialism, 1876–1910* (Berkeley and Los Angeles: University of California Press, 1967), pp. 75–77; Spencer J. Palmer, ed., *Korean-American Relations: Documents Pertaining to the Far Eastern Diplomacy of the United States,* 2 vols. (Berkeley and Los Angeles: University of California Press, 1963), pp. 307–309; Nagao Ariga, "Diplomacy," in *Japan by the Japanese: A Survey by Its Highest Authorities,* ed. Alfred Stead (London: William Heinemann, 1904), p. 203; William E. Henthorn, *A History of Korea* (New York: Free Press, 1971), p. 221.

31. Harrington, *God, Mammon, and the Japanese,* pp. 141–156, 211–221.

32. Tyler Dennett, *Americans in Eastern Asia: A Critical Study*

of the Policy of the United States with Reference to China, Japan, and Korea in the 19th Century (New York: Barnes & Noble, 1941, reprint of 1922 Macmillan edition), pp. 461–462, 477–478, 495.

33. Sill to Skerrett, enclosed in Sill to Gresham, June 1, 1894, Dispatches from United States Ministers to Korea, vol. 11, National Archives Record Group 59, hereafter cited as Korea Dispatches.

34. Impey to Day, Aug. 15, 1894, Area Files of the Naval Records Collection, Area 10, National Archives Record Group 45, hereafter cited as Area 10 File.

35. Skerrett to Sill, enclosed in Sill to Gresham, June 1, 1894, Korea Dispatches, vol. 11.

36. *Report of the Secretary of the Navy,* 1894, pp. 3–11; view of Skerrett, in Allen to Rockhill, July 3, 1894, Rockhill Papers.

37. Gresham to Herbert, attached to Ye Lung-loo to Gresham, June 1, 1894, Area 10 File. For a life of Herbert, see Hugh Bernard Hammett, "Hilary Abner Herbert: A Southerner Returns to the Union" (Ph.D. dissertation, University of Virginia, 1969).

38. George F. Parker, *Recollections of Grover Cleveland* (New York: Century, 1909), p. 384; *New York Tribune,* June 2, 1894.

39. Sill to Skerrett, June 8, 1894, enclosed in Skerrett to Herbert, June 8, 1894, Area 10 File; *New York Tribune,* June 15, 1894.

40. Dun to Gresham, June 15, 1894, Japan Despatches, vol. 66. For the view that Mutsu easily impressed Dun with his sincerity, see Treat, *United States and Japan,* 2: 462–463.

41. Sill to Gresham, June 18, 1894, Korea Dispatches, vol. 11.

42. Tateno to Uhl, June 23, 1894, Notes from Japan, vol. 5.

43. Uhl to Sill, June 22, 1894, Diplomatic Instructions of the Department of State, Korea, vol. 1, National Archives Record Group 59, hereafter cited as Korea Instructions.

44. *F.R.U.S., 1894,* p. ix.

45. Andrew Malozemoff, *Russian Far Eastern Policy, 1881–1904, with Special Emphasis on the Causes of the Russo-Japanese War* (Berkeley and Los Angeles: University of California Press, 1958), pp. 53–54.

46. Sill to Gresham, June 25, 1894, Korea Dispatches, vol. 11; Sill to Skerrett, June 25, 1894, Area 10 File; Korean minister to Gresham, July 5, 1894, Notes from the Korean Legation in the United States to the Department of State, vol. 1, National Archives Record Group 59, hereafter cited as Notes from Korea; see also Read to Uhl, July 7, 1894, Consul Tientsin, vol. 4.

47. *New York Times,* June 30, 1894; also Gresham to Dun, June 29, 1894, Diplomatic Instructions of the Department of State, Japan, vol. 4, National Archives Record Group 59, hereafter cited as Japan Instructions.

48. Typescript of Tateno-Gresham talks, July 7, 1894, Notes from Japan, vol. 5.

49. Gresham to Dun, July 7, 1894, Japan Instructions, vol. 4.

50. *San Francisco Examiner,* July 18, 1894; *New York Tribune,* July 19, 1894; *Hartford Post,* July 20, 1894; identical views in *Emporia Gazette* (Kansas), July 19, 1894, and *Philadelphia Inquirer,* July 19, 1894.

51. Sill to Dun, July 19, 1894, Sill to Gresham, July 24, 1894, Korea Dispatches, vol. 11.

52. Sill to Day, July 23, 1894, Area 10 File.

53. Day to Sill, July 20, 1894, ibid.

54. Sill to Gresham, July 24 and 26, 1894, Korea Dispatches, vol. 11.

55. Sill to Day, Aug. 1, 1894, Day to Sill, Aug. 3, 1894, Area 10 File; G. F. Elliott, "Marines in Seoul, Korea," in *Report of the Secretary of the Navy, 1895,* pp. 523–529; also see Deck Log Book of the USS *Baltimore,* National Archives Record Group 24; Day to Sill, July 24, 1894, Area 10 File.

56. *F.R.U.S., 1894,* p. ix.

2. Neutrality

1. Denby to Gresham, Mar. 16, 1894, China Despatches, vol. 94.

2. Read to Uhl, July 22, 1894, Consul Tientsin, vol. 4; Jernigan to Uhl, July 23, 1894, Despatches from U.S. Consuls in Shanghai, vol. 42, National Archives Record Group 59, hereafter cited as Consul Shanghai; Sill to Gresham, July 26, 1894, Korea Dispatches, vol. 11; Denby Jr. to Gresham, July 27, 1895, China Despatches, vol. 95.

3. Sill to Day, July 28, 1894, Day to Herbert, July 28, 1894, Elliott to Day, July 28, 1894, all in Area 10 File.

4. Cecil Spring-Rice, a secretary in the British legation in Washington during 1894, described the Washington summer in a letter to Mrs. Theodore Roosevelt, Aug. 24, 1894, quoted in *The Letters and Friendships of Sir Cecil Spring-Rice: A Record,* 2 vols., ed. Stephen Gwynn (Boston and New York: Houghton Mifflin, 1929), 1: 160.

5. Denby to Gresham, July 31, 1894, China Despatches, vol. 95; Gresham to Denby, Aug. 3, 1894, Gresham Papers.

6. Von Hanneken's report, in Sill to Gresham, Aug. 3, 1894, Korea Dispatches, vol. 11; Denby Jr. to Gresham, July 28, 1894, China Despatches, vol. 95.

7. *Chicago Tribune,* July 28, 1894.

8. *Atlanta Constitution,* July 29, 1894; *Chicago Tribune,* July 30, 1894; *New York Tribune,* Aug. 1 and 3, 1894.

9. Predictions that the *Kowshing* affair would mean immediate

declarations of war, in Denby Jr. to Gresham, July 28, 1894, China Despatches, vol. 95.

10. John Bassett Moore, *A Digest of International Law,* 8 vols. (Washington: Government Printing Office, 1906), 7: 860.

11. Miyaoka to Gresham, Aug. 1, 2, and 4, 1894, Notes from Japan, vol. 5.

12. Chang Yin-huan to Bayard, Aug. 12, 1894, Bayard Papers, Library of Congress; Denby Jr. to Gresham, Aug. 4, 1894, China Despatches, vol. 95.

13. Moore, *Digest of International Law,* 7: 8; Te-kong Tong, *United States Diplomacy in China, 1844–60* (Seattle: University of Washington Press, 1964), provides a good summary of early diplomacy.

14. Moore, *Digest of International Law,* 7: 417, 680–683.

15. *San Francisco Examiner,* Aug. 4, 1894; *Pacific Commercial Advertiser,* Aug. 20, 1894.

16. *Commercial and Financial Chronicle,* Aug. 6, 1894; *Richmond State,* Aug. 7, 1894; *New York Tribune,* Sept. 6, 1894; McIvor to Uhl, Aug. 13,1894, Despatches from U.S. Consuls in Kanagawa, vol. 20, National Archives Record Group 59.

17. *Journal of the Knights of Labor,* Aug. 2 and 9, 1894; also, *United Mine Workers' Journal,* Aug. 2, 1894.

18. *Advocate of Peace,* Sept. 1894; *Staunton Weekly News* (Virginia), Aug. 9, 1894; *Boston Globe,* Aug. 13, 1894.

19. *New York Tribune,* Aug. 28, 1894; *San Francisco Examiner,* Aug. 6 and 9, 1894; *Springfield Republican,* Oct. 6, 1894; *New York Herald,* Oct. 6, 1894; *New York Tribune,* Aug. 3 and 5, 1894, and Dec. 2 and 21, 1894.

20. Warrington F. Eastlake and Yamada Yoshi-aki, *Heroic Japan* (Yokohama, 1896), pp. 439, 442; James Allan, *Under the Dragon Flag: My Experiences in the Chino-Japanese War* (New York: Stokes, 1898); Hosea Ballou Morse to Inspector General of Chinese Customs Robert Hart, Aug. 6, 1894, and Oct. 26, 1894, Morse Collection, Houghton Library, Harvard University; Denby Jr. to Gresham, Sept. 8, 1894, China Despatches, vol. 96.

21. Gwynn, ed., *Letters of Cecil Spring-Rice,* 1: 159; *New York Tribune,* Sept. 24, 1894.

22. *New York Tribune,* Aug. 27, 1894; *Atlanta Constitution,* Aug. 6, 1894; *San Francisco Examiner,* Aug. 8, 16, 17, 1894.

23. Dun to Gresham, Dec. 7, 1894, Japan Despatches, vol. 68. Complete discussion in Jeffery M. Dorwart, "Providence Conspiracy of 1894," *Rhode Island History* 32 (Aug. 1973): 91–96.

24. Aldrich to Chinese minister, Aug. 27, 1894, Wilde to Tateno, July 3, 1894, both enclosed in Dun to Gresham, Dec. 7, 1894, Japan Despatches, vol. 68.

25. Foster to Moore, Sept. 5, 1894, Brazilian minister to Foster, Sept. 5, 1894, both enclosed in ibid. Months later Mrs. Foster

denied that her husband knew anything about the plot or had ever heard of the conspirators, *New York Tribune,* Mar. 8, 1895.

26. Moore to Wilde, Sept. 13, 1894, Wilde to Moore, Sept. 17, 1894, enclosed in Dun to Gresham, Dec. 7, 1894, Japan Despatches, vol. 68.

27. File enclosed in ibid.

28. Smithers quoted in Sakuye Takahashi, *Cases on International Law during the Chino-Japanese War* (Cambridge University Press, 1899), p. 68; *New York Times,* Nov. 9, 1894.

29. Gresham to Dun, Nov. 8, 1894, Japan Instructions, vol. 4; Read to Uhl, Feb. 9, 1895, Consul Tientsin, vol. 5; Carpenter to Herbert, Feb. 19, 1895, Area 10 File.

30. *San Francisco Examiner,* Aug. 9, 1894; *New York Tribune,* Aug. 14 and 18, 1894.

31. Gresham to Dun, Aug. 30, 1894, Japan Instructions, vol. 4.

32. Moore, *Digest of International Law,* 7: 856–858; Henry F. Merrill, an employee of the Chinese Customs Service, discussed trade obstructions in Merrill to Hart, Aug. 25, 1895, "Merrill Transcript," 3: 34–35, Morse Collection.

33. Gresham to Denby Jr., Aug. 15, 1894, Sept. 17 and 28, 1894, Diplomatic Instructions of the Department of State, 1801–1906: China, vol. 5, National Archives Record Group 59, hereafter cited as China Instructions; Denby Jr. to Gresham, Aug. 10, 1894, China Despatches, vol. 95. As Gresham had hoped, American commerce escaped search and seizure, though French, German, British, and Scandinavian registry vessels were stopped by Oriental navies during the war, Takahashi, *International Law,* pp. 16–18.

34. Pauncefote to Gresham, Aug. 7, 1894, Gresham Papers; *New York Tribune,* Aug. 5, 6, and 15, 1894; *San Francisco Examiner,* Aug. 22, 1894; *New Orleans Picayune,* Aug. 5, 1894.

3. Good Offices

1. Moore, *Digest of International Law,* 7: 7–8.

2. Gresham to Denby Jr., July 26, 1894, China Instructions, vol. 5; Gresham to Dun, July 26, 1894, Japan Instructions, vol. 4; Tsungli-yamen to Denby Jr., July 28, 1894, China Despatches, vol. 95; Yang to Gresham, July 30, 1894, Notes from the Chinese Legation in the United States to the Department of State, vol. 3, National Archives Record Group 59, hereafter cited as Notes from China; Gresham to Yang, July 31, 1894, Notes to Foreign Legations in the United States from the Department of State: China, vol. 1, National Archives Record Group 59, hereafter cited as Notes to China; also, Treat, *United States and Japan,* 2: 459, 463, 471–490.

3. Denby Jr. to U.S. consular officials in China, July 31, 1894, China Despatches, vol. 95; Uhl to Denby Jr., Sept. 14, 1894, countermanded in Gresham to Denby, Dec. 20, 1894, China Instructions, vol 5.

4. Denby Jr. to Tsungli-yamen, Aug. 1, 1894, Komura Jutaro to Denby Jr., Aug. 1, 1894, China Despatches, vol. 95.

5. Read to Uhl, Aug. 2, 1894, Consul Tientsin, vol. 4; Denby Jr. to Gresham, Aug. 14, 1894, China Despatches, vol. 95.

6. Jernigan to Uhl, Aug. 4, 1894, Consul Shanghai, vol. 42.

7. McIvor to Uhl, Aug. 6, 1894, Consul Kanagawa, vol. 20; Treat, *United States and Japan,* 2: 474, stated that "The Department files do not record a single instance in which the American officials had to intervene to protect Chinese subjects."

8. McIvor to Uhl, Aug. 6, 1894, Consul Kanagawa, vol. 20; State Department denial in Gresham to Denby Jr., Sept. 18, 1894, China Instructions, vol. 5.

9. Denby Jr. to Gresham, Aug. 8, 1894, Tsungli-yamen to Denby Jr., Aug. 6, 1894, China Despatches, vol. 95.

10. Jernigan to Uhl, Aug. 21, 1894, Consul Shanghai, vol. 42; Tsungli-yamen to Chinese minister [translation], Aug. 18, 1894, Notes from China, vol. 3.

11. Gresham to Denby Jr., Aug. 18, 1894, China Instructions, vol. 5.

12. Denby Jr. to Gresham, Aug. 21 and 27, 1894, China Despatches, vol. 95.

13. Gresham to Denby Jr., Aug. 29, 1894, China Instructions, vol. 5.

14. Denby Jr. to Gresham, Aug. 26 and 31, 1894, China Despatches, vol. 95.

15. Gresham to Denby Jr., Aug. 31, 1894, ibid.

16. Denby Jr. to Gresham, Sept. 1, 1894, ibid.

17. Wilson, *China,* pp. 20–23.

18. Child to Uhl, Sept. 3, 1894, Despatches from U.S. Consuls in Hankow, vol. 7, National Archives Record Group 59.

19. Denby Jr. to Gresham, Sept. 5, 1894, China Despatches, vol. 96.

20. Child to Uhl, Sept. 3, 1894, Consul Hankow, vol. 7; Jernigan to Uhl, Sept. 21, Consul Shanghai, vol. 42.

21. Denby Jr. to Gresham, Aug. 27, 1894, China Despatches, vol. 95.

22. Rockhill to Alfred E. Hippisley, Oct. 30, 1894, Rockhill Papers.

23. *New Orleans Picayune,* Sept. 7, 1894; also *Staunton Weekly News,* Sept. 6, 1894; *New York Tribune,* Sept. 5, 1894.

24. Hippisley to Rockhill, Jan. 26, 1895, Rockhill Papers.

25. Jernigan to Uhl, Sept. 21 and Oct. 22, 1894, Consul Shanghai, vol. 42.

26. Quoted in Gresham to Denby Jr., Oct. 20 and 30, 1894, China Instructions, vol. 5.

27. Jernigan to Uhl, Oct. 9, 22, and Nov. 2, 1894, Consul Shanghai, vol. 42.

28. Julian Ralph, *The Making of a Journalist* (New York: Harper & Bros., 1903), pp. 129–130.

29. Henry Cabot Lodge, *Selections from the Correspondence of Theodore Roosevelt and Henry Cabot Lodge, 1884–1918*, 2 vols. (New York: Scribner's, 1925), 1: 140; Ralph, *Journalist,* p. 130.

30. *Congressional Record,* 53 Cong., 3 sess., 27 (Dec. 5, 1894): 39; also see George E. Paulsen, "Secretary Gresham, Senator Lodge, and American Good Offices in China, 1894," *Pacific Historical Review* 36 (May 1967): 123–142.

31. Gresham, *Gresham,* p. 765.

32. Gresham to Morgan, Gresham to Sherman, Dec. 6, 1894, Gresham Papers.

33. *Congressional Record,* 53 Cong., 3 sess., 27 (Dec. 5, 1894): 39, 41.

34. Ibid.

35. Gresham to Denby, Dec. 26, 1894, Gresham Papers.

36. Gresham to Yang, Nov. 30 and Dec. 27, 1894, Notes to China, vol. 1.

37. Yang to Gresham, Dec. 6, 1894, Notes from China, vol. 3.

38. Yang to Gresham, Dec. 31, 1894, ibid.

39. Clipping from *New York Evening Post,* Dec. 3, 1894, signed "Justice to Gresham" with inked corrections presumably by Gresham, Gresham Papers; also see "Secretary Gresham's Surrender of Japanese Refugees," *Literary Digest* 10 (Dec. 8, 1894): 151–152.

40. *New York Tribune,* Dec. 11, 1894; *New York World,* Jan. 17, 1894.

41. Denby to Gresham, Dec. 31, 1894, China Despatches, vol. 97.

42. Jernigan to Uhl, Jan. 23, 1895, Consul Shanghai, vol. 42.

4. Gunboat Diplomacy

1. Denby Jr. to Gresham, Aug. 18 and 24, 1894, China Despatches, vol. 95; Denby Jr. to Gresham, Aug. 13, 1894, Read to Uhl, Aug. 15, 1894, both in Area 10 File; also see Dugald Christie, *Thirty Years in the Manchu Capital in and around Moukden in Peace and War* (New York: McBride, Nast, 1914), pp. 87–89.

2. Chapin to Smith, Sept. 18, 1894, North China Mission, vol. 18, Noble to Smith, Jan. 11, 1895, North China Mission, vol. 20,

Archives of the American Board of Commissioners for Foreign Missions, Houghton Library, Harvard University, hereafter cited as ABCFM; *New York Herald,* Oct. 6, 1894.

3. Sill to Gresham, Sept. 26, 1894, Korea Dispatches, vol. 11; *Atlanta Constitution,* Aug. 1 and 5, 1894; *New York Tribune,* Aug. 2, 5, and 8, 1894; *Chicago Inter-Ocean,* Aug. 2, 1894.

4. Gresham to Dun, Aug. 15, 1894, Japan Instructions, vol. 4.

5. Gresham to Cleveland, Oct. 2, 1894, Cleveland Papers, Library of Congress.

6. Gresham to Herbert, Aug. 21, 1894, Day to Carpenter, Aug. 29, 1894, Carpenter to commander of the *Concord,* Aug. 1, 1894, Area 10 File. Also see Jeffery M. Dorwart, "The United States Navy and the Sino-Japanese War of 1894–1895," *The American Neptune* 34 (July 1974): 211–218.

7. *Boston Globe,* Apr. 3, 1899; *New York Times,* Apr. 3, 1899.

8. Cooperative policy discussed in William Reynolds Braisted, *The United States Navy in the Pacific, 1897–1909* (Austin: University of Texas Press, 1958), p. 16; *New York Herald,* Oct. 5, 1894.

9. Carpenter to Fremantle, Nov. 7, 1894, Carpenter to Herbert, Nov. 10, 1894, Fremantle (commander-in-chief of *Centurion*) to Carpenter, Nov. 14, 1894, Pauncefote to Gresham, Dec. 14, 1894, Area 10 File; Ann Parry, *The Admirals Fremantle* (London: Chatto & Windus, 1971).

10. Folger to secretary of the navy, Jan. 22, 1895, Carpenter to secretary of the navy, Jan. 22 and 29, 1895, Area 10 File; Log Book of the *Yorktown,* July 1, 1894–Dec. 31, 1894; Denby to Gresham, Jan. 21, 1895, China Despatches, vol. 97; *North China Herald,* 54 (Feb. 1, 1895): 156.

11. Carpenter to A. R. Donnelly, Feb. 3, 1895, Donnelly to Carpenter, Feb. 2, 1895, Area 10 File.

12. Donnelly to Carpenter, Feb. 6, 1895, Coffin to Carpenter, Feb. 8, 1895, Rev. Charles A. Killie to commanding officer, rescue vessel, Feb. 10 and 12, 1895, ibid.

13. Carpenter to secretary of the navy, Feb. 13, 1895, Carpenter to U.S. consular agents, Jan. 26, 1895, Folger to Carpenter, Feb. 5, 1895, ibid.

14. Sill to Carpenter, Sept. 17, 1894, Carpenter to Sill, Sept. 18 and 25, 1894, ibid.

15. Carpenter to Sill, Oct. 25, 1894, Sill to Carpenter, Oct. 26, 1894, ibid.

16. Sill to Gresham, Nov. 2 and Dec. 4, 1894, Korea Dispatches, vol. 11; Sill to Uhl, Jan. 17, 1895, Despatches from U.S. Consuls in Seoul, National Archives Record Group 59, vol. 1.

17. Sill to Gresham, Mar. 16, 1895, Sill to Folger, Mar. 13, 1895, Korea Dispatches, vol. 11; also, Sill to Coffin, Dec. 4, 1894, Area 10 File.

18. See Elliott to commanding officer of *Baltimore,* Dec. 4, 1894, Area 10 File.

19. McAdoo to Carpenter, Nov. 19, 1894. Day to Hayward, Macfarland, Newell, Schon, Morris, enclosed in Carpenter to Sill, Jan. 11, 1895, statement of Rose Ely Moore signed by Horace N. Allen, enclosed in Carpenter to secretary of the navy, Jan. 23, 1895, Sill to Carpenter, Jan. 14, 1895, Day to Carpenter, Jan. 12, 1895, forwarded to secretary of the navy, Jan. 23, 1895, ibid.

20. Carpenter to secretary of the navy, Nov. 29, 1894; Emory to secretary of the navy, No. 21, 1894, Emory to Carpenter, Mar. 27, 1895, ibid.; Log Book of the steamer *Petrel,* Aug. 1, 1894–Feb. 7, 1895, National Archives Record Group 24; Dun to Gresham, Mar. 9, 1895, Japan Despatches, vol. 68; also see Isabella L. Bishop, *Korea and Her Neighbours,* 2 vols. (London: John Murray, 1898), 1: 216.

21. Consul W. R. Carles to Goodrich, Dec. 6 and 7, 1894, Goodrich to Carpenter, Dec. 7 and 13, 1894, Area 10 File.

22. Craig to Carpenter, Dec. 31, 1894, Craig to Carpenter, Jan. 21, 1895, Craig to commander-in-chief, Chefoo, Jan. 25, 1895, Craig to Carpenter, Jan. 28, 1895, Fowler to Carpenter, Jan. 30, 1895, ibid.

23. Jernigan to Uhl, Mar. 18, 1895, Consul Shanghai, vol. 42; Craig to Carpenter, Feb. 9 and 19, 1895, Area 10 File.

24. *Staunton Weekly News,* Feb. 7, 1895; also, *New York Tribune,* Feb. 4, 1895.

25. Denby Jr. to Gresham, Oct. 3, 1894, China Despatches, vol. 96; *New York Herald,* Sept. 29, 1894; Ament to Smith, Oct. 2, 1894, North China Mission, vol. 17, ABCFM.

26. Denby Jr. to Gresham, Oct. 8 and 15, 1894. China Despatches, vol. 96.

27. Denby to Gresham, Oct. 31, 1894, ibid.

28. Carpenter to Denby, Nov. 19, 1894, Carpenter to Secretary of the Navy, Nov. 29 and Dec. 1, 1894, Area 10 File; Gresham to Denby, Nov. 8, 1894, China Instructions, vol. 5; Denby to Gresham, Nov. 23, 1894, China Despatches, vol. 96.

29. *Report of the Secretary of Navy,* 1895–96, pp. 526–527.

30. Carpenter to commander of the *Monocacy,* Dec. 4, 1894, Area 10 File.

31. Ament to Judson Smith, Dec. 17, 1894, North China Mission, vol. 17, ABCFM; also see Henry D. Porter, *William Scott Ament* (New York: Fleming H. Revell, 1911), p. 128.

32. Denby to Gresham, Dec. 18 and 22, 1894, China Despatches, vol. 97; Denby to Carpenter, Dec. 22, 1894, Area 10 File; Gresham to Denby, Dec. 19, 1894, China Instructions, vol. 5.

33. Translation of cable from Tsungli-yamen to Yang, forwarded to Gresham, Dec. 28, 1894, Notes from China, vol. 3; also, Denby to Gresham, Dec. 29, 1894, China Despatches, vol. 97.

34. Gresham to Denby, Dec. 27, 1894, China Instructions, vol. 5.

35. Denby to Gresham, Dec. 29, 1894, and Jan. 3, 1895, China Despatches, vol. 97; also, Gresham to Denby, Jan. 1, 1895, China Instructions, vol. 5; Carpenter to Denby, Jan. 6, 1895, Area 10 File.

36. Denby to Gresham, Feb. 18, 1895, China Despatches, vol. 97; Read to Uhl, Feb. 9 and 18, 1895, Consul Tientsin, vol. 5; Impey to Elliott, Feb. 6, 1895, Elliott to Impey, Feb. 19, 1895, Area 10 File.

37. Gresham to Denby, Feb. 28, 1895, China Instructions, vol. 5.

5. Peacemaker

1. *Advocate of Peace* 56 (Sept. 1894): 206,(Nov. 1894): 257; *San Francisco Examiner,* Oct. 20, 1894; *Richmond State,* Oct. 4, 1894.

2. Quoted in *New York World,* Dec. 25, 1894.

3. *New York Tribune,* Nov. 14, 1894; also, *Boston Daily Globe,* Nov. 15, 1894.

4. *Review of Reviews* 10 (Dec. 1894): 600,(Sept. 1894): 251; also see Marilyn Blatt Young, *The Rhetoric of Empire: American China Policy, 1895–1901* (Cambridge: Harvard University Press, 1968), p. 23.

5. *New York Herald,* Oct. 6, 1894.

6. Richard Watson Gilder, *Grover Cleveland, a Record of Friendship* (New York: Century, 1910), p. 121.

7. Gresham to Cleveland, Oct. 12, 1894, Gresham Papers.

8. Cleveland to Gresham, Oct. 12, 1894, ibid.

9. Denby Jr. to Gresham, Oct. 23, 1894, Denby to Gresham, Oct. 31 and Nov. 4, 1894, China Despatches, vol. 96.

10. Gresham to Denby, Nov. 24, 1894, China Instructions, vol. 5; Denby to Gresham, Nov. 19, 1894, China Despatches, vol. 96.

11. Gresham to Denby, No. 6 and 8, Dec. 26, 1894, China Instructions, vol. 5.

12. Gresham to Denby, Nov. 8, 1894, ibid.; also see Denby to Gresham, Nov. 19, 1894, China Despatches, vol. 96.

13. Quoted in Kurino to Gresham, Nov. 10, 1894, Notes from Japan, vol. 5; Denby to Gresham, Nov. 16, 1894, China Despatches, vol. 96.

14. Kurino to Gresham, Nov. 18, 1894, Notes from Japan, vol. 5.

15. Dun's note of Nov. 15, quoted in Gresham to Dun, Dec. 22, 1894, Japan Instructions, vol. 4; Mutsu to Kurino, Kurino to Gresham, Nov. 17, 1894, Notes from Japan, vol. 5; Gresham to Yang, Nov. 20, 1894, Notes to China, vol. 1; *New York Tribune,* Nov. 22, 1894.

16. *Philadelphia Ledger,* quoted in *Public Opinion* 17 (Nov. 29, 1894): 839.

17. *New Orleans Picayune,* Nov. 20, 1894; *Indianapolis Journal, Detroit News,* quoted in *Public Opinion* 17 (Nov. 29, 1894): 839; *Atlanta Constitution,* Nov. 22, 1894; also see *Syracuse Post, New York Herald, Philadelphia Press, Baltimore American,* quoted in *New York Tribune,* Nov. 23, 1894.

18. Denby to Gresham, Nov. 16 and 22, 1894, China Despatches, vol. 96.

19. Detring to Read to Uhl, Nov. 26, 1894, Consul Tientsin, vol. 4; *New York Tribune,* Nov. 28 and 30, 1894; *Springfield Republican,* Dec. 9, 1894; Dun to Gresham, Dec. 7, 1894, Japan Despatches, vol. 68; Kenneth E. Folsom, *Friends, Guests, and Colleagues: The Mu-Fu System in the Late Ch'ing Period* (Berkeley and Los Angeles, University of California Press, 1968), pp. 153–154.

20. Denby to Gresham, Jan. 14, 1895, China Despatches, vol. 97.

21. Denby to Gresham, Dec. 1, 1894, ibid.; for the view that Denby served only as an adviser on "nonsubstantive" matters, see Young, *Rhetoric of Empire,* pp. 31–32, 241.

22. Denby to Gresham, Dec. 1, 1894, enclosed in Denby to Gresham, Dec. 8, 1894, China Despatches, vol. 97; see also Denby to Gresham, Dec. 5, 1894, Cleveland Papers; Gresham to Denby, Dec. 2, 1894, China Instructions, vol. 5; Dun to Gresham, Dec. 7, 1894, Dun to Denby, Dec. 18, 1894, Dun to Gresham, Dec. 20, 1894, Japan Despatches, vol. 68.

23. Denby to Gresham, Dec. 13, 20, 21, and 24, 1894, Jan. 4, 1895, China Despatches, vol. 97; Denby to Dun, Dec. 12, 1894, Dun to Denby, Dec. 20, 1894, Dun to Gresham, Dec. 20, 1894, Dun to Gresham, Dec. 26 and 28, 1894, Japan Despatches, vol. 68.

24. Dun to Gresham, Dec. 28, 1894, Jan. 7, 1895, Japan Despatches, vol. 68.

25. Denby to Gresham, Dec. 29, 1894, China Despatches, vol. 97; Denby to Carpenter, Dec. 22, 1894, Area 10 File.

26. Denby to Gresham, Dec. 31, 1894, Jan. 2, 1894, China Despatches, vol. 97.

27. Denby to Gresham, Jan. 17, 1895, ibid.

28. Gresham to Denby, Feb. 7, 1895, China Instructions, vol. 5.

29. Denby to Gresham, Feb. 9, 1895, China Despatches, vol. 97.

30. Gresham to Bayard, Dec. 24, 1894, letterbook, vol. 43, Gresham Papers.

31. Young, *Rhetoric of Empire,* pp. 27–30; see also Denby Jr. to Gresham, Apr. 14, 1894, China Despatches, vol. 94; Read to Uhl, Apr. 14, 1894, Consul Tientsin, vol. 4; John W. Foster, *Diplomatic Memoirs,* 2 vols. (Boston: Houghton Mifflin, 1910), 2: 95.

32. Gresham to Bayard, Dec. 24, 1894, Gresham Papers.

33. Resolution, quoted in Gresham, *Gresham,* 2: 788.

34. *Congressional Record,* 53 Cong., 3 sess., 27: 621–622.

35. Foster, *Diplomatic Memoirs,* 2: 114; Denby to Gresham, Jan. 23, 1895, China Despatches, vol. 97; also, Uhl to Denby, Jan. 25, 1895, China Instructions, vol. 5.

36. Dun to Gresham, Feb. 2, 3, 4, 5, and 15, 1895, Japan Despatches, vol. 68; Denby to Gresham, Feb. 5, 1895, China Despatches, vol. 97; Abercrombie to Uhl, Feb. 23, 1895, Despatches from U.S. Consuls in Nagasaki, National Archives Record Group 59, vol. 6.

37. *Boston Globe,* Feb. 5, 1895.

38. Denby to Gresham, Feb. 4 and 14, 1895, China Despatches, vol. 97; Dun to Gresham, Feb. 5, 1895, Japan Despatches, vol. 68.

39. Denby to Gresham, Feb. 17, 1895, China Despatches, vol. 97; also, Read to Uhl, Feb. 18, 1895, Consul Tientsin, vol. 5; Gresham to Denby, Feb. 18, 1895, China Instructions, vol. 5.

40. Denby to Gresham, Feb. 17 and 20, 1895, China Despatches, vol. 97.

41. Denby to Gresham, Feb. 23 and 26, 1895, ibid.

42. Denby to Gresham, Feb. 26, 1895, ibid.

43. Denby to Gresham, Mar. 5, 1895, ibid.

44. *Staunton Weekly News,* Mar. 21, 1895; Read to Uhl, Mar. 12, 1895, Consul Tientsin, vol. 5.

45. Denby to Gresham, Mar. 23, 1895, China Despatches, vol. 98.

46. Ibid.

47. Gresham to Yang, Mar. 30, 1895, Notes to China, vol. 1; Yang to Gresham, Mar. 29, 1895, Notes from China, vol. 3; Dun to Gresham, Mar. 28, 1895, Japan Despatches, vol. 68.

48. Foster, *Diplomatic Memoirs,* 2: 134; Folsom, *Friends, Guests, and Colleagues,* pp. 153–155.

49. Foster, *Diplomatic Memoirs,* 2: 126–133. The Japanese negotiators also employed an American during the peace talks, Henry W. Denison of Vermont, who had worked for the Japanese Foreign Office since 1880. Denison kept Foster informed of Japanese demands, although his part in the peace conference remained more subtle than Foster's; Treat, *United States and Japan,* 2: 518, 521, 528; Dulles, *Yankee and Samurai,* p. 155.

6. The Pigtail War

1. *New York Herald,* quoted in *Public Opinion* 17 (Aug. 2, 1894): 417; also see *San Francisco Examiner,* July 29, 1894, *New Orleans Picayune,* July 28, 1894, *New York Times,* July 28, 1894.

2. *San Francisco Examiner,* Sept. 29, 1894; for similar views see

Pacific Commercial Advertiser, July 17, 1894, *New York Tribune,* July 2, 1894, *Boston Globe,* July 23, 1894.

3. *Atlanta Constitution,* July 24 and 26, 1894; also see *Boston Globe,* July 25, 26, and 29, 1894, *New York Tribune,* July 25, 1894.

4. Lafcadio Hearn, *Kokoro: Hints and Echoes of Japanese Inner Life* (Boston and New York: Houghton Mifflin, 1899), p. 9; similar views in *New York Tribune,* July 29, 1894, *St. Paul Pioneer Press,* quoted in *Public Opinion* 17 (Aug. 2, 1894): 417.

5. Hearn, *Kokoro; Dictionary of American Biography,* 7: 484–486.

6. Helen H. Gardener, "Japan, Our Little Neighbor in the East," *Arena* 11 (Jan. 1895): 178; *New York Tribune,* July 29, 1894.

7. B. O. Flower, "Justice for Japan," *Arena* 10 (July 1894): 225–236.

8. *San Francisco Examiner,* July 26 and 29, 1894, Aug. 2 and 12, 1894; *Atlanta Constitution,* July 27, 1894; *New York Tribune,* July 25 and 27, 1894, Aug. 12, 1894; *Boston Globe,* July 27, 1894.

9. Julian Ralph, *Alone in China and Other Stories* (New York: Harper & Bros., 1897), pp. 19–20; Ralph to Secretary of War Daniel S. Lamont, Aug. 4 and 10, 1894, Lamont Papers, Library of Congress.

10. *Atlanta Constitution,* Aug. 27, 1894.

11. *Boston Globe,* Aug. 2, 1894; *New York Tribune,* Aug. 14, 1894.

12. Read to Uhl, Feb. 16, 1894, Consul Tientsin, vol. 4.

13. *New York Tribune,* Aug. 6, 1894; *Atlanta Constitution,* Aug. 4, 1894; *Boston Globe,* Aug. 3, 1894; *Pacific Commercial Advertiser,* Sept. 6, 1894; John Russell Young, "Li Hung Chang: A Character Sketch of the Premier of China," *Review of Reviews* 10 (Oct. 1894): 386–395. Also see Stanley Spector, *Li Hung-chang and the Huai Army: A Study in Nineteenth-Century Chinese Regionalism* (Seattle: University of Washington Press, 1964); Folsom, *Friends, Guests, and Colleagues.*

14. Hearn to Basil Hall Chamberlain, June 8, 1894, Hearn Papers, Clifton Waller Barrett Collection, Alderman Library, University of Virginia, Charlottesville; *Dictionary of American Biography,* 9: 257–258.

15. *New York Tribune,* Aug. 1, 3, and 5, 1894; also, *Atlanta Constitution,* July 29, 1894; *Chicago Tribune,* July 30, 1894.

16. Gwynn, ed., *Letters of Cecil Spring-Rice,* 1: 164. Mary A. Holbrook, an American Board teacher in Kobe, reported Japanese mail tampering to James Levi Barton, foreign corresponding secretary of the ABCFM, Sept. 17, 1894, Japan Mission, vol. 21, ABCFM. Also see *New York Herald,* Oct. 6, 1894; *Atlanta Constitution,* Sept. 25, 1894.

17. Gresham, *Gresham,* 2: 789.

18. *Boston Globe,* Nov. 21, 1894; *New York Tribune,* Oct. 21, 1894; Yang to Gresham, Sept. 22, 1894, Notes from China, vol. 3.

19. Kurino Shinchiro, "The Oriental War," *North American Review* 159 (Nov. 1894): 529–536. See also Michitaro Hisa, "The Significance of the Japan-China War," *Forum* 18 (Oct. 1894): 216–227; Kuma Oishi, "The Causes Which Led to the War in the East," *Arena* 10 (Nov. 1894): 726–727; Midori Komatz, "Japan, Its Present and Future," *Arena* 12 (Mar. 1895): 1–9.

20. Ibid. Also see "The Japanese Press on the War." *Literary Digest* 9 (Sept. 8, 1894): 564–565; Trumbull White, *The War in the East, Japan, China, and Corea* (Philadelphia, 1895), p. 13.

21. Ralph, *Journalist,* p. 102; also, *Atlanta Constitution,* Aug. 26, 1894.

22. *New York Tribune,* Aug. 2, 1894.

23. *Springfield Republican,* Aug. 2, 1894.

24. *Newark Advertiser,* quoted in *New York Tribune,* Aug. 4, 1894; *New York Times,* Aug. 1, 1894; *Springfield Republican,* July 30, 1894; *Commercial and Financial Chronicle* 59 (Aug. 4, 1894): 173; also see Jack Hammersmith, "The Sino-Japanese War, 1894–5: American Predictions Reassessed," *Asian Forum* 4 (Jan.–Mar. 1972): 48–58.

25. "Notes on the Japan-China War," *Office of Naval Intelligence Reports,* General Information Series No. 14 (Washington: Government Printing Office, 1895), p. 29.

26. Ralph, *Alone in China,* p. 22.

27. *Atlanta Constitution,* Aug. 26, 1894.

28. *Atlantic Monthly,* Dec. 1887, p. 725, quoted in John W. Foster, *American Diplomacy in the Orient* (Boston: Houghton Mifflin, 1903), p. 342.

29. *Atlanta Constitution,* July 29, 1894.

30. Ibid., Aug. 8, 1894; also, *Louisville Courier-Journal,* quoted in *New York Tribune,* Aug. 4, 1894, *Philadelphia Press,* quoted in *New York Tribune,* Aug. 2, 1894, *Richmond State,* Aug. 15, 1894.

31. James Creelman, *On the Great Highway* (Boston: Lothrop, 1901), pp. 32–54; *New York World,* Sept. 28, 1894; see also Eastlake and Yamada, *Heroic Japan,* pp. 26–40.

32. *New York Tribune,* Sept. 18 and 19, 1894.

33. *Public Opinion* 17 (Sept. 27, 1894): 620.

34. Learned to Barton, Sept. 17, 1894, Japan Mission, vol. 22, ABCFM.

35. *New York World,* Sept. 28, 1894; *Boston Globe,* Sept. 20, 1894.

36. McGiffen to Lieutenant Dunby (?), Nov. 13, 1894, Area 10 File; also see Philo Norton McGiffen, "The Battle of the Yalu: Personal Recollections by the Commander of the Chinese Ironclad *Chen Yuen,*" *Century Magazine* 50, new series 28 (Aug. 1895): 585–604.

37. Jukichi Inouye, "The Naval Battle of Haiyang," in *The Japan-China War* (Yokohama: Kelly & Walsh, n.d.), pp. 1–25; John L. Rawlinson, *China's Struggle for Naval Development, 1839–1895* (Cambridge: Harvard University Press, 1967), pp. 168–195, 247–258, 260–261; Rear Admiral S. S. Robison and Mary L. Robison, *A History of Naval Tactics from 1530 to 1930* (Annapolis: The United States Naval Institute, 1942), p. 739; Vice Admiral G. A. Ballard, *The Influence of the Sea on the Political History of Japan* (London: John Murray, 1921), pp. 145–153.

38. Denby Jr. to Gresham, Sept. 19, 1894, China Despatches, vol. 96; Impey to the secretary of the navy, Sept. 19, 1894, Area 10 File; Sill to Gresham, Sept. 20 and 21, 1894, Korea Dispatches, vol. 11.

39. Herbert to Carpenter, Sept. 24, 1894, Area 10 File.

40. Hobson to his uncle Richmond, Nov. 1895, correspondence, 1894–1933, box 45, Hobson Papers, Library of Congress.

41. Roosevelt to Herbert, Dec. 12, 1894, correspondence, 1878–1931, part 1, Herbert Papers, University of North Carolina Library; Walter R. Herrick Jr., *The American Naval Revolution* (Baton Rouge: Louisiana State University Press, 1966), pp. 176–178.

42. "Notes on Life of Phil. Norton McGiffen, 1860–1897," compiled by Richard Harding Davis, Barrett Collection, Alderman Library, University of Virginia, Charlottesville; William Ferdinand Tylor, *Pulling Strings in China* (London: Constable, 1929), pp. 57–58.

43. Hilary A. Herbert, "The Fight off the Yalu River," *North American Review* 159 (Nov. 1894): 513–528; Japanese translation of article in Herbert Papers.

44. *Report of the Secretary of the Navy,* 1895, p. xvii.

45. Ibid., 1894, p. 12.

46. Ibid., p. 17; also, Hammett, "Hilary Abner Herbert," pp. 228–231.

47. *Report of the Secretary of the Navy,* 1895, pp. 513–514, 169; Frank Marble, "The Battle of Yalu," United States Naval Institute *Proceedings,* 2: 479–522; Robison and Robison, *Naval Tactics,* pp. 737–744; Walter LaFeber, *The New Empire: An Interpretation of American Expansion, 1860–1898* (Ithaca: Cornell University Press, 1963), p. 312.

48. *New Orleans Daily Picayune,* Nov. 12, 1894.

49. *New York Tribune,* Sept. 24, 1894; Mahan to Clarke, Sept. 30, 1894, special correspondence, box 3, Mahan Papers, Library of Congress.

50. *New York Tribune,* Sept. 21, 1894; clipping from *Boston Advertiser,* n.d., Herbert scrapbook, 1893–94, Herbert Papers; A. T. Mahan, "Lessons from the Yalu Fight," *Century Magazine* 50, new series 28 (Aug. 1895): 629–632.

51. *New York Times,* Feb. 13, 1915, p. 9; Creelman, *On the*

Great Highway, pp. 8off; Jeffery M. Dorwart, "James Creelman, the *New York World* and the Port Arthur Massacre," *Journalism Quarterly* 50 (winter 1973): 697–701.

52. Sill to Gresham, Feb. 20, 1895, Korea Dispatches, vol. 11; also see Gresham to Sill, Apr. 1, 1895, Korea Instructions, vol. 1.

53. *New York World,* Sept. 25 and 28, 1894.

54. *World* to House, Nov. 23, 1894; Col. Yamanouchi to House, Dec. 1, 1894, Clemens-House Collection, Alderman Library University of Virginia.

55. Creelman, *On the Great Highway,* pp. 80–81; Allan, *Under the Dragon Flag,* pp. 38–42; Carpenter to Herbert, Nov. 29, 1894, Area 10 File.

56. Creelman, *On the Great Highway,* p. 109; Allan, *Under the Dragon Flag,* pp. 66–67.

57. *New York World,* Dec. 11, 20, 23, and 24, 1894.

58. *New York Tribune,* Nov. 24, 25, 29, and 30, 1894; *New York World,* Nov. 30, Dec. 9 and 11, 1894.

59. *New York World,* Jan. 9, 12, and 20, 1895, Feb. 11, 1895; Frederic Villiers, "The Truth about Port Arthur," *North American Review* 160 (Mar. 1895): 325–330.

60. *World* to House, Dec. 13, 1894, Clemens-House Collection; *New York World,* Dec. 17 and 18, 1894.

61. *New York World,* Dec. 23, 1894.

62. Ibid., Dec. 21, 1894.

63. Ibid., Dec. 22, 1894; also, *Atlanta Constitution,* Jan. 6, 1895, *New York Tribune,* Dec. 20, 1894.

64. *Philadelphia Record,* quoted in "The Massacre at Port Arthur," *Public Opinion* 17 (Dec. 27, 1894): 939–940.

65. Dun to Gresham, Dec. 20, 1894, Japan Despatches, vol. 68.

66. Dun to Gresham, Dec. 20, 1894, and Jan. 7, 1895, ibid.

67. See Dun to Gresham, Jan. 17, 1895, and Feb. 15, 1895, ibid.; Inouye, "The Fall of Weihaiwei," in *Japan-China War,* pp. 1–26; copy of Oyama telegram reporting Weihaiwei battle, Feb. 6, 1895, Notes from Japan, vol. 5; Carpenter to secretary of the navy, Feb. 7, 1895, Area 10 File; Denby to Gresham, Feb. 8, 1895, China Despatches, vol. 97.

68. See Carpenter to secretary of the navy, Feb. 13, 1895, Area 10 File; Dun to Gresham, Feb. 15 and 27, 1895, Japan Despatches, vol. 68; Deck Log Book of the USS *Charleston,* Feb. 17–22, 1895, National Archives Record Group 24.

69. *Journal of the American Medical Association* 23 (July–Dec. 1894): 995; *Pacific Commercial Advertiser,* Oct. 15, 1894, p. 8; Nagao Ariga, *The Red Cross Society of Japan* (St. Louis: Universal Exposition, 1904), pp. 5–6.

70. Gravatt to Herbert, Mar. 30, 1895, Area 10 File; C. U. Gravatt, "Method of Caring for Wounded in Field and Hospital of Chinese and Japanese Armies," *Proceedings Sixth Annual Meeting*

Military Surgeons (May 1896), pp. 137–143; Uhl to Dun, May 16, 1895, Japan Instructions, vol. 4; Dun to Gresham to Lamont, Feb. 28, 1895, Japan Despatches, vol. 68; Colonel Dallas Bache, "Synopsis of a Report on the Medico-Military Arrangements of the Japanese Army in the Field, 1894–1895," *Proceedings Sixth Meeting*, pp. 159–183; W. F. Arnold, "Notes on Gunshot Wounds in Cases of Chinese Soldiers," *Annual Report of the Surgeon-General, U.S. Navy* (Washington: Government Printing Office, 1895), pp. 190–194.

71. W. A. P. Martin, *A Cycle of Cathay, or China, South and North with Personal Reminiscences*, 2nd ed. (New York: Revell, 1897), p. 405.

72. *New York Tribune*, Dec. 7, 1894; *Springfield Republican*, Dec. 17, 1894.

73. Rev. J. H. DeForest, "The Political Preparation for Christ in the Far East," *Missionary Herald* 91 (June 1895): 232.

74. *Journal of the American Medical Association* 23 (July-Dec. 1894): 995.

7. Reviving Interest in East Asia

1. Charles Denby, *China and Her People*, 2: 17.

2. Theodore Ayrault Dodge, "The Eastern War, and After: A Military Study," *Forum* 18 (Nov. 1894): 320.

3. Lucius H. Foote, "The War in the Orient," *Overland Monthly* 24, 2nd series (Nov. 1894): 523–528.

4. Denby to Gresham, Nov. 16, 1894, China Despatches, vol. 96; see J. O. P. Bland and E. Backhouse, *China under the Empress Dowager* (London: Heinemann, 1910), pp. 98–99.

5. *New York Tribune*, Oct. 29, 1894; Merrill to Hart, Nov. 5, 1894, "Merrill Transcript," Morse Collection.

6. Ament to Smith, Dec. 17, 1894, North China Mission, vol. 17, ABCFM.

7. *New York Evening Sun*, quoted in *Pacific Commercial Advertiser*, Nov. 1, 1894; Denby to Gresham, Nov. 16, 1894, China Despatches, vol. 96.

8. Dodge, "Eastern War," p. 315.

9. Ibid.; also, McClellan, *Heathen Chinee*, pp. 82–83.

10. Sternburg to Roosevelt, July 30, 1895, Theodore Roosevelt Papers, Library of Congress.

11. *Richmond State*, Oct. 13, 1894; *Atlanta Constitution*, Nov. 2, 1894; *New York Tribune*, Sept. 28 and Nov. 17, 1894; Brown, *Mastery*, p. 507; "Is Infanticide Practised in China?" *Catholic World* 60 (Mar. 1895): 781; *Brooklyn Standard-Union*, quoted in

Richmond State, Oct. 4, 1894; *Staunton Weekly News,* Nov. 8, 1894; *New York Herald,* Oct. 2, 1894; *New York World,* Sept. 28, 1894.

12. Augustine Heard, Durham W. Stevens, and Howard Martin, "China and Japan in Korea," *North American Review* 159 (Sept. 1894): 310–312.

13. Ibid., p. 316.

14. Dodge, "Eastern War," pp. 315–319.

15. *Atlanta Constitution,* Jan. 7, 1894; *Richmond State,* Nov. 28, 1894; Foote, "War in Orient," p. 524; Lafcadio Hearn, *Editorials from the Kobe Chronicle,* ed. Makoto Sangu (Tokyo: The Hoku-seido Press, 1960), pp. 31–34.

16. *New York Tribune,* Sept. 28, 1894.

17. MacArthur, quoted in *Pacific Commercial Advertiser,* Oct. 19, 1894; *New Orleans Picayune,* Nov. 12, 1894.

18. Heard, Stevens, and Martin, "China and Japan," pp. 300–301.

19. Rockhill to Hippisley, Oct. 30, 1894, Rockhill Papers.

20. Learned to Barton, Nov. 24, 1894, Japan Mission, vol. 22, ABCFM.

21. *Advocate of Peace* 56 (Sept. 1894): 204.

22. William Elliot Griffis, "American Relations with the Far East," *New England Magazine* 9, new series (Nov. 1894): 272; also *Missionary Review of the World* 18 (Feb. 1895): 137.

23. Read to Uhl, Nov. 14, 1894, Consul Tientsin, vol. 4; Jernigan to Uhl, Oct. 9, 1894, Consul Shanghai, vol. 42.

24. Rockhill to Hippisley, Oct. 30, 1894, Rockhill Papers.

25. *F.R.U.S., 1894,* p. xi.

26. Gresham to Dun, July 16, 1894, Gresham to Morgan, Jan. 10, 1895, Gresham Papers.

27. *American Federationist* 1 (May 1894): 50; Dodge, "Eastern War," p. 322; *Richmond State,* Oct. 31, 1894; also, Miller *Unwelcome Immigrant.*

28. Paul Hibbert Clyde, *United States Policy toward China: Diplomatic and Public Documents, 1839–1939* (Durham: Duke University Press, 1940), pp. 140–158; *F.R.U.S., 1894,* p. 177; George E. Paulsen, "The Gresham-Yang Treaty," *Pacific Historical Review* 36 (Aug. 1968): 281–297.

29. Kurino to Gresham, Sept. 18, 1894, Notes from Japan, vol. 5.

30. Reid to Mills, Oct. 18, 1894, Reid to Col. John Hay, Oct. 10, 1894, box 40, vol. 49, Whitelaw Reid Papers, Library of Congress.

31. *New York Tribune,* Sept. 22, 1894.

32. *New York Herald,* Sept. 26, 1894; *New Orleans Picayune,* Dec. 10, 1894.

33. Denby to Gresham, Apr. 25, 1895, China Despatches, vol. 98; Dun to Gresham, May 18, 1895, Japan Despatches, vol. 68; *Documentary History of the Peace Negotiations between China and*

Japan, March–April 1895 (Tientsin: Tientsin Press, 1895), pp. 1–29.

34. Dun to Gresham, Apr. 16 and 18, 1895, Japan Despatches, vol. 68; Denby to Gresham, Apr. 29, 1895, China Despatches, vol. 98.

35. Denby to Gresham, May 13, 1895, China Despatches, vol. 98; Dun to Gresham, Apr. 25 and 26, 1895, Japan Despatches, vol. 68.

36. Gresham, *Gresham,* p. 788.

37. Denby to Gresham, Mar. 21 and 26, 1895, China Despatches, vol. 98.

38. Sill to Gresham, Mar. 1, 1895, Korea Dispatches, vol. 11.

39. Jernigan to Uhl, May 2 and 11, 1895, Consul Shanghai, vol. 42.

40. Allen to Rockhill, May 2, 1895, Rockhill Papers; Read to Uhl, May 9, 1895, Consul Tientsin, vol. 5.

41. Foster, *Diplomatic Memoirs,* 2: 147–149.

42. Ibid.

43. Denby to Gresham, May 4 and 6, 1895, China Despatches, vol. 98; Dun to Gresham, May 9, 1895, Japan Despatches, vol. 68.

44. Denby to Gresham, May 7, 1895, Japan Despatches, vol. 68.

45. Eastlake and Yamada, *Heroic Japan,* pp. 522–525; Denby to Dun, May 8, 1895, Denby to Gresham, May 9, 1895, Japan Despatches, vol. 68; Denby to Gresham, May 8, 1895, China Despatches, vol. 98.

46. Sheffield to Smith, May 14, 1895, North China Mission, vol. 21, ABCFM; Jernigan to Uhl, May 11, 1895, Consul Shanghai, vol. 42.

47. Satoh to Griffis, May 24, 1895, Griffis Papers, Special Collections, Rutgers University Library, New Brunswick.

48. Mutsuhito to Cleveland, June 18, 1895, Notes from Japan, vol. 5.

49. Gresham, *Gresham,* p. 789.

50. For further discussion, see Jeffery M. Dorwart, "Walter Quintin Gresham and East Asia, 1894–1895: A Reappraisal," *Asian Forum* 5 (Jan.–Mar. 1973): 55–63.

Essay on Selected Sources

This essay includes only the major sources used to discuss the American response to the Sino-Japanese War of 1894–1895; other material can be found in the footnotes.

Diplomatic and naval records located in the National Archives, Washington, D.C., provide the framework for this study. The General Records of the Department of State (Record Group 59) contain a large body of information on United States diplomacy toward the war. Dispatches from the U.S. ministers in China, Japan, and Korea; Diplomatic Instructions from the Department of State to its representatives in East Asia; and Notes from the Chinese, Japanese, and Korean legations in the United States to the Department of State contribute useful information. Dispatches from United States consuls in Chefoo, Foochow, Hankow, Kanagawa, Nagasaki, Ningpo, Shanghai, and Tientsin often reveal conditions at the treaty ports and attitudes of local diplomats unavailable in other reports.

For the naval reaction to the conflict, the Area 10 File covering East Asia in the Area Files of the Naval Records Collection (Record Group 45) and Deck Log Books of the United States Navy ships in the war zone (Record Group 24) prove particularly helpful on diplomatic as well as military matters.

Published government reports which discuss the war include *Notes on the War between China and Japan* (1896) compiled by the military information division of the Adjutant General's Office, *Annual Reports of the Secretary of the United States Navy* (1894–1896), *Annual Reports of the Surgeon-General, U.S. Navy* (1895), *Notes on the*

Year's Naval Progress (1895) issued by the Office of Naval Intelligence, and *Papers Relating to the Foreign Relations of the United States* (1893–1895).

Several prominent Americans commented extensively on the Sino-Japanese War in their personal correspondences. The Walter Quintin Gresham Letterbooks in the Library of Congress, the William Woodville Rockhill Collection in the Houghton Library of Harvard University, the William Elliot Griffis Papers in the Special Collections of the Rutgers University Library at New Brunswick, Horace N. Allen's "Korean Collection" in the New York Public Library, and the Hilary Abner Herbert Papers in the Southern Historical Collection of the University of North Carolina Library are all rich sources. Volumes of letters on the war can be found in the Archives of the American Board of Commissioners for Foreign Missions, Houghton Library, Harvard University, and in Foreign Missions Correspondence and Reports, Presbyterian Church in the U.S.A., Presbyterian Historical Society, Philadelphia. Scattered references to the conflict exist in the Papers of Thomas Francis Bayard, Richmond P. Hobson, Alfred Thayer Mahan, Louis Theodore Michener, Richard Olney, Whitelaw Reid, Grover Cleveland, Theodore Roosevelt, and John Russell Young, all in the Library of Congress. Also helpful were the papers of Lafcadio Hearn, Edward Howard House, Richard Harding Davis, and Rev. Randolph Bryan Grinnan, on deposit in the University of Virginia Library, Charlottesville.

There are a few memoirs by Americans interested in the war which refer to the Sino-Japanese struggle. John W. Foster, *Diplomatic Memoirs,* 2 vols. (Boston: Houghton Mifflin, 1910) remains the best source for American participation in the peace talks at Shimonoseki. Charles Denby, *China and Her People: Being the Observations, Reminiscences, and Conclusions of an American Diplomat,* 2 vols. (Boston: L. C. Page, 1906) is disappointing on the minister's contributions. James Creelman, *On the Great Highway: The Wanderings and Adventures of a Special Correspondent* (Boston: Lothrop, 1901) presents a colorful account of the journalist's war experiences. Julian Ralph, *Alone in China and Other Stories* (New York: Harper & Bros., 1897) and *The Making of a Journalist* (New York and London: Harper & Bros., 1903) discuss his observations of East Asia during the conflict. W. A. P. Martin, *A Cycle of Cathay, or China, South and North with Personal Reminiscences,* 2nd ed. (New York: Revell, 1897) refers to the war. The adventures of an Anglo-American gun-runner are recounted in James Allan, *Under the Dragon Flag: My Experiences in the Chino-Japanese War* (New York: Stokes, 1898).

Editorial and journalistic opinion is treated in the text and footnotes. The major newspapers used to discover prevailing attitudes and views include the *Atlanta Constitution, Boston Globe, Chicago Tribune, New Orleans Picayune, New York Tribune, New York World, Pacific Commercial Advertiser* (Honolulu), *Richmond State, San Francisco Examiner,* and *Springfield* (Mass.) *Republican.* Many other papers were surveyed, and all followed the tone set by the above carefully scanned sources. Magazine articles on the Sino-Japanese War often appeared during late 1894 and early 1895 in the *North American Review, Forum, Arena, Overland Monthly, Commercial and Financial Chronicle, Literary Digest, Public Opinion, Century Magazine, Missionary Review of the World,* and the American *Review of Reviews.*

There is nothing on American diplomacy toward the Sino-Japanese War to compare with Lillian Ota Dotson's treatment of Chinese and Japanese policies in "The Sino-Japanese War of 1894–95: A Study in Asian Power Politics" (Ph.D. dissertation, Yale University, 1951). The best account of U.S. conduct during the war remains Payson J. Treat, *Diplomatic Relations between the United States and Japan, 1853–1895,* 3 vols. (Gloucester: Peter Smith, 1963, reprint of 1932 Stanford University Press edition), while Tyler Dennett, *Americans in Eastern Asia: A Critical Study of the Policy of the United States with Reference to China, Japan, and Korea in the 19th Century* (New York: Macmillan, 1922) describes American good offices during the war. More recently an excellent introductory chapter in Marilyn Blatt Young, *The Rhetoric of Empire: American China Policy, 1895–1901* (Cambridge: Harvard University Press, 1968), shows how the war stimulated investment schemes and forced the U.S. government to define its interests in East Asia. In his opening chapter, Thomas J. McCormick, *China Market: America's Quest for Informal Empire, 1893–1901* (Chicago: Quadrangle, 1967), sees the war as a catalyst for America's drive for informal economic empire in China, while Walter LaFeber, *The New Empire: An Interpretation of American Expansion, 1860–1898* (Ithaca: Cornell University Press, 1968), argues that the Cleveland administration feared European intervention during the war and sought to preserve an open door to trade by employing diplomacy to end the fighting.

Several scholarly articles on American diplomacy and public attitudes toward the Sino-Japanese War have appeared. George E. Paulsen recognizes Gresham's contributions in "Secretary Gresham, Senator Lodge, and American Good Offices in China, 1894," *Pacific Historical Review,* vol. 36 (May 1967), and "The Gresham-Yang Treaty," *Pacific Historical Review,* vol. 36 (Aug. 1968). Also helpful are Jack Hammersmith, "The Sino-Japanese War, 1894–5: American Predictions Reassessed," *Asian Forum,* vol. 4 (Jan.–Mar. 1972), and Thomas L. Hardin, "American Press and Public Opinion in the First Sino-Japanese War," *Journalism Quarterly,* vol. 50 (Spring 1973).

Biographies of Americans involved in the diplomacy of the Asian conflict of 1894–1895 furnish additional material. There is no scholarly study of Secretary of State Gresham, although Matilda Gresham, *Life of Walter Quintin Gresham, 1832–1895,* 2 vols. (Chicago: Rand McNally, 1919), presents letters on his East Asian policies unavailable in the Gresham Papers. Secretary of the Navy Herbert, the only other cabinet officer to devote much attention to the war, receives full coverage in Hugh Bernard Hammett, "Hilary Abner Herbert: A Southerner Returns to the Union" (Ph.D. dissertation, University of Virginia, 1969). Allan Nevins, *Grover Cleveland: A Study in*

Courage (New York: Dodd, Mead, 1966) remains the best biography of the president. Asian expert Rockhill is discussed in Paul A. Varg, *Open Door Diplomat: The Life of W. W. Rockhill* (Urbana: University of Illinois Press, 1952), while John William Cassey, "The Mission of Charles Denby and International Rivalries in the Far East, 1885–1898" (Ph.D. dissertation, University of Southern California, 1959), details the minister's long career at the Peking legation. Fred Harvey Harrington, *God, Mammon, and the Japanese: Horace N. Allen and Korean-American Relations, 1884–1905* (Madison: University of Wisconsin Press, 1944), discusses Allen's many activities in Korea. Minister Sill's contributions are surveyed in Shirley W. Smith, "John M. B. Sill," in *Michigan and the Cleveland Era: Sketches of University of Michigan Staff Members and Alumni Who Served the Cleveland Administrations, 1885–89, 1893–97,* ed. Earl D. Babst and Lewis Vander Velde (Ann Arbor: University of Michigan Press, 1948). There are no studies of Minister Dun, Consul General Jernigan, and other minor diplomats.

Index